#OOTD OUTFIT OF THE DAY

Sew & Style

Make Your Dream Wardrobe with Angela

Angela Lan

stashBOOKS®

an imprint of C&T Publishing

Text copyright © 2016 by Angela Lan

Photography and artwork copyright © 2016 by C&T Publishing, Inc.

Publisher: Amy Marson

Creative Director: Gailen Runge

Art Director: Kristy Zacharias

Editors: Liz Aneloski and
Katie Van Amburg

Technical Editors: Alison M. Schmidt
and Helen Frost

Cover/Book Design: Page+Pixel

Production Coordinator: Zinnia Heinzmann

Production Editors: Joanna Burgarino,
Katie Van Amburg, and Jessie Brotman

Illustrators: Jenny Davis and
Zinnia Heinzmann

Photo Assistant: Sarah Frost

Style photography by Meo Baaklini
and instructional photography by
Diane Pedersen, unless otherwise noted

Published by Stash Books, an imprint of C&T Publishing, Inc., P.O. Box 1456, Lafayette, CA 94549

Library of Congress Cataloging-in-Publication Data
Names: Lan, Angela, author.
Title: #OOTD (outfit of the day) sew & style : make your dream wardrobe with
 Angela / Angela Lan.
Other titles: #OOTD (outfit of the day) sew and style | Outfit of the day sew
 & style | Outfit of the day
Description: Lafayette, CA : Stash Books, an imprint of C&T Publishing, Inc.,
 [2016] | Audience: Ages 12-16._ | Includes index.
Identifiers: LCCN 2015039094 | ISBN 9781617451362 (soft cover)
Subjects: LCSH: Sewing--Juvenile literature. | Dressmaking--Juvenile
 literature. | Dress accessories--Juvenile literature. | Girls'
 clothing--Juvenile literature. | Fashion design--Juvenile literature.
Classification: LCC TT712 .L36 2016 | DDC 646.4--dc23 LC record
available at http://lccn.loc.gov/2015039094

Printed in China

10 9 8 7 6 5 4 3 2 1

DEDICATION

To my family. I love you forever. XOXO

ACKNOWLEDGMENTS

Thank you to everyone who told me I could do it; those who stuck with me through thick and thin and gave me words of encouragement. More specifically, a huge thank-you to the following:

All my friends for the laughter and fun we've had throughout the years. It's been great, and I hope to continue to keep our friendship alive during the years to come.

Ms. Irma, for proofreading the drafts of this book and frequently correcting my sentences, even when I think they're fine.

Michelle Reiss, for being an awesome teacher and always helping me with whatever I decide to make, though half of the time you don't know what I'm doing.

Alex Anderson, for introducing me to C&T Publishing and encouraging me to follow my passion.

Dawn and Eddie Leone, Ms. Chase, Ms. Lisa, Julianne Knapp, and all my teachers for the support in life along the way.

Fabric.com, for providing all the gorgeous fabrics and supplies used in this book. I hope to work together again in the future.

The team at C&T—thank you for making this book come true and for giving me a chance. Roxane, Liz, Alison, Kristy, Diane, and Sarah, you were a pleasure to work with. That goes for all the other wonderful people who also worked on this project; I wish I could say a huge thank-you in person. You're all amazing! :)

My family: Daddy and Cynthia for constantly supporting me, 24 hours a day, 7 days a week. Love you both. Mommy, who told me that I could do it, even when I didn't think I could. Thank you for supporting everything I do. I know I'm not the typical kid and I'm particularly different, but I'm truly grateful. I couldn't have done any of this without you. I promise I'll make you proud. Love you!

CONTENTS

INTRODUCTION

Fashion has evolved over the years, and it's never been so focused on the individual as it is now. Clothes aren't just pieces of cloth anymore; rather, they are extensions of the wearer's personality. Each and every person is developing his or her own style and way of dressing.

At the same time, sewing is being embraced by a new, younger generation. It's hard enough for us teens to find clothes that fit our bodies *and* our styles! What's even harder is knowing that we might outgrow our new clothes in just a matter of months. What teen wouldn't want the ability to turn designs into real-life items or alter that cute, too-small tee with needle and thread?

When you combine fashion and sewing, you get fashion sewing, a modern and creative way to express yourself one step further by creating the clothes you wear. I'm sure there are clothes you've pictured in your head that you just can't find at the mall. Maybe you have a whole "dream wardrobe" you've been unable to find or buy. When you learn fashion sewing, all those clothes you've been dreaming of can become real-life garments—made by *you*! When you're the designer, you can create exactly what you want.

I'm guessing that's why you decided to pick up this book. You're at the right place, whether you're an avid DIY-er, fashion lover, or even just a teenager who's eager to try something new.

With fast fashion these days, it's hard not to get caught up in what others are wearing and what *they* think looks good. Clothing that *you* love and that will last is invaluable, especially when you designed and made it yourself. By starting with some basic designs, adding little touches, and then modifying the designs little by little, you can turn these designs into many variations that'll help you create key pieces to build a whole new wardrobe.

My goal isn't to teach you how to make fancy ball gowns that you'll only wear once before you outgrow them. I want to teach you how to create clothes that you'll want to wear—and can wear—on an everyday basis. And, yes, I'll teach you some tricks to make sure your garments look professional and store-bought!

We'll cover everything from developing a style to sewing zippers. If you love colors and fun designs, girl, go do your thing! Make what you want to wear according to your style and love the end product. It's all about *your* style and experimenting with different fabrics until you've developed a wardrobe you love.

Telling everyone who compliments you on your new outfit that you made it yourself will definitely be your proudest moment out of the entire process—but nothing is more creatively satisfying than having the ability to make any garment you can dream of.

Ready to design, sew, and make your dream wardrobe come true?

Most important, remember to have fun. I wish you a happy journey!

XX, ANGELA

How to Use This Book

When I first started sewing, I wanted to do everything at once and go straight to formal dresses with lots of detailing. But when I did, the "little things" were often overlooked, and I never really understood what I was doing. Suddenly my work started falling apart (literally and figuratively!) and I had no idea what to do.

By taking things one step at a time, you'll get a solid foundation on garment construction. Then you can move onto more complicated designs without getting overwhelmed by the process and the huge amount of concepts to learn at once.

Knowing *why* clothes are made a certain way helps a lot as you move into more complicated designs. Therefore, I've explained the "whys" to garment construction—as in why they are sewn specific ways—in an attempt to help you really understand the concepts.

As with any other hobby or profession, we'll start with the basics. Each chapter teaches you a little more about sewing, with a project at the end of each to help you show off your skills. I highly recommend practicing the techniques shown in the how-to pages on scrap fabric before moving on. It's a skill-building process; the projects will get more advanced as you progress throughout the book.

By the end, I hope you will have learned enough to be designing and making your own clothes.

And as cliché as this sounds, I truly believe that you can do it. The best way to learn is by doing, so let's get started!

THE BASICS

Garment sewing is sometimes thought to be a scary world, when it really is a world of choices and fun. We'll start easy and learn about the fabric choices you have when making your own garments, as well as some basic stitches both on the sewing machine and by hand. You'll also build a handy sewing kit with all the essentials needed for sewing. At the end, I'll show you how to make a beautiful infinity scarf. Let's get started!

Fabric

The world of fabric is filled with gorgeous options, from wool to lace to silk and much more. Before heading off to the fabric store, make sure you know what you need and what you're looking for. The choices you have are endless, so it's easy to get overwhelmed in the middle of it all. But don't worry: with a little fabric knowledge, you'll soon be on your way!

The types of fabrics are usually split into two categories: woven and knit. There are many more, but for the sake of simplicity, we're going to be working with these two. I'll explain them both in more detail and show samples of the different types of fabrics that fall under each category later.

GRAIN

Fabric grain is the direction the threads or yarns run in a piece of fabric. Grain affects the drape and fit of the finished clothing. If the grain is off (that is, the threads/yarns are running slanted or in the wrong direction), then the garment may hang weirdly on the body, resulting in an unflattering look.

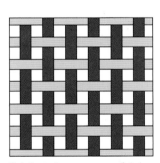

Fabric grain on a *woven* fabric

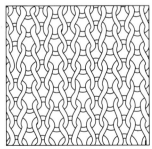

Fabric grain on a *knit* fabric

All fabrics that are cut off the roll or bolt (the cardboard that fabric is wrapped around / sold on in stores) look something like the illustration below. The fabric is folded in half, with the selvages together and the cut edge running vertically.

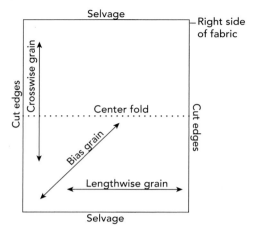

When you unfold the fabric, it looks like this, with selvages now running on both sides of the fabric.

- The **lengthwise grain** runs parallel to the selvages. There's very little stretch in this direction.

- The **crosswise grain** runs from selvage to selvage. This is where the fabric was cut to give you the amount you needed. In woven (nonstretchy) fabrics, there is more "give" (meaning the fabric will stretch, or "give" a little bit) in this direction than the lengthwise grain. In knit (stretchy) fabrics, this is where the fabric stretches the most. Knit clothing is cut with this direction running horizontally across your body.

- The **fabric bias** (or **bias grain**) is a 45° diagonal from the selvage. In woven fabrics, this is the only place where there's a bit of stretch, whereas in knits, it's about the same as the crosswise grain. When woven fabrics are cut on the bias, they can go around curves much more fluidly because of the "give."

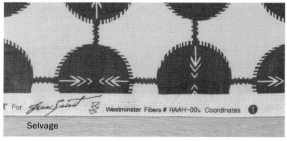

Fabric selvages (the uncut, already-finished edges of fabric) usually have small holes punctured in them or information about the fabric.

While this may not matter at first, it's very important to understand the grain of fabric when working with patterns. You'll learn more in Chapter 2 (page 40).

FABRIC LABELS

When you buy fabric in-store, you'll usually see a sticker on the end of the bolt (the cardboard the fabric is wrapped around and sold on) stating what the fabric is made of, its care instructions, how wide the fabric is, and how much it costs per yard. Later in the book, you'll learn more about fabric content and fibers (page 12), but you should write this information down when you buy the fabric. Also take note of the care instructions, so you'll know how to care for the finished garment. The clothes you make don't come with labels or tags, so the sticker on the bolt is your best bet.

The number of inches written on the sticker is how wide the fabric is. It's usually 45˝ or 60˝ wide. Some projects have specific requirements on the width, so pay attention to the fabric requirements. For example, the DIY Skater Skirt (page 69) requires a 60˝-wide fabric; otherwise, there won't be enough fabric to make the skirt.

If you are buying fabric online, all of this information should be included in the product description.

Price   Fabric content/ Type of fabric   Fabric width

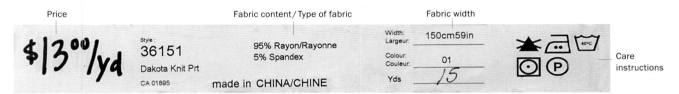

Care instructions

Fabric bolt sticker

Item Number 0404881

Country of Origin Made in the USA or Imported

Contents 100% Cotton

Fabric Weight Very Lightweight ❓

Width 52"

Brand Free Spirit

Designer Amy Butler

Reorderable ❓

Glossary of Fabric Terms >

Collections   Amy Butler Bright Heart   Amy Butler Bright Heart Voile

Description: Designed by Amy Butler for Free Spirit, this cotton print voile fabric has a soft hand, excellent drape, and is slightly sheer. This fabric is perfect for apparel such as blouses, tunics and dresses. The color palette includes navy blue, lilac, magenta, pink and orange.

Washing Instructions ❓ : Machine Wash Cold/ Tumble Dry Low

Online fabric description from Fabric.com

Fibers and Fabric Content

FABRIC FIBERS

There are so many different ways to describe a piece of fabric other than its color or print. Later in this book, we will discuss how fabric is made (woven or knit) and the names we can call them (like voile, denim, or leather, page 14). We can also describe fabric by their **fibers**, otherwise known as **fabric content**: cotton, polyester, wool, and so on. Fabric, both knit and woven, is made from threads. Fibers are what make the threads.

Each type of fiber has its own properties. Some are more breathable and softer than others, while others have more "give" to them. It's important to know what your fabric is made of, so you can be sure to buy fabric that will last and is suitable for the climate and wear and tear you're going to be putting it through. You don't want to be wearing a stuffy top during the summer or a coat with no warmth or durability during the chilly seasons.

To find the content of a fabric, look at the top of a bolt of fabric where the price and care label are. It will usually say what percentage of a certain type of fiber it has. You can also find this information on ready-to-wear clothing tags.

By looking at this label, I know that this fabric is 95% rayon and 5% spandex. But what does that mean? Take a look at the following guide.

WHAT FIBERS SHOULD I USE?

As you can see, all fibers have their pros and cons. By choosing a blend of fibers, you may be able to avoid the cons, but I suggest you choose based on the climate where you live. If you live in a place where it's hot and moist all year around, linen will be a fiber you'll want to use again and again. On the other hand, if you live in Winter Wonderland, wool may be the best choice for keeping you warm.

Go with your instincts and use your senses to find the perfect fiber or blend for you. When you go shopping for fabric, feel the fabric. Is it something you would like to wear on your body? Is it soft enough to your liking? Do you like the feel of it? When in doubt, take a look at the label and double-check the characteristics listed on the next page. If you're still unsure, go for a blend of two fibers so you'll have the best of both.

MOST COMMON FABRICS AND THEIR CHARACTERISTICS

COTTON

Made from the cotton plant, **cotton** is a natural fiber that has become very popular in clothing today. It's great for year-round wear and is mostly found in T-shirts because of how comfortable it is. Fabrics made from cotton start at affordable prices, so it's also perfect for making clothes. Just be aware that some cottons can be very stiff, so I suggest buying fabric in person to make sure you like the feel of it. Also, prewashing (page 20) softens the fabric. I like to look for fabrics that are a cotton blend, meaning they are made from a mix of cotton and another fiber.

POLYESTER

Polyester is a synthetic (human-made) fiber, so it's less expensive than cotton. It doesn't wrinkle easily and comes in a variety of different fabrics with varied weights and textures, from satin to chiffon to fleece, so it's often used in clothing. Polyester is best used when it's blended with another fiber, creating a poly-blend, which gives the fabric more breathability than when it's used by itself. Poly-cotton or poly-rayon blends are some of my favorite fabrics to work with.

WOOL

Wool is a natural fiber, made from the fleece of sheep. It can be made into thread for fabric or yarn for knitting and crocheting. Fabrics can be all-wool or a blend. By itself, it may be a little pricey, but wool blends can be much more affordable. Wool is great for winter wear in clothing such as coats or skirts. Wool is perfect for keeping warm while still being able to breathe. Be aware, though, that some wools can be extremely itchy. I'm sure we've all had that super-coarse, scratchy sweater!

SPANDEX/ LYCRA

Spandex is another synthetic fiber. It is commonly used in swimsuits and active wear because of its ability to stretch while still being able to spring back into shape. Super-skinny jeans often have some spandex in order to give them their stretch. Spandex is never used on its own; it is always combined in amounts from 1% to 15% with another fiber such as polyster or cotton. A touch of spandex is great when making something fitted that needs a little or a lot of stretch.

RAYON

Rayon is generally considered a synthetic fiber but is not entirely human-made. It is made from cellulose, which comes from wood pulp from trees. Because of this, it acts a lot like natural fibers. Rayons have very good drape and are soft to wear. They are a great alternative to silks because of their drape and breathability, but be aware that they do not stand up to heavy wear. Drapey poly-rayon knits or rayon challises are my favorite fabrics containing rayon.

SILK

Silk fiber comes from the cocoons of silkworms and makes luxurious fabric. Silk is a treat to wear but can be pricey. It's quite comfortable and can keep you cool in the summer and warm in the winter. It is mostly chosen for its sheen. Silk comes in all kinds of prints, dyes, and textures. When silk is woven into a slippery fabric like satin or charmeuse, it can be a little harder to work with and requires precision and skill. Most types of silk fabrics (chiffon, georgette, charmeuse, and more) are made in polyester as well.

LINEN

Linen is a natural fiber that comes from the flax plant. It has great durability and is super soft. Linens are easy to sew with and come in all sorts of colors. With the right drape, they are great for making garments. Linen is perfect for hot and moist climates because of its absorbency and breathability. However, they tend to wrinkle easily—but perhaps you want that worn-in look?

Fabric Types

WOVENS

Woven fabrics, or "wovens" as I like to call them, are the fabrics without stretch. Have you ever made one of those loop pot holders where you kept on going "over, under, over, under"? That's how woven fabrics are made. They're formed from threads going the opposite direction of one another, weaving up and down. The threads can start to  unravel with wear and tear, so wovens need to be treated at the edges to prevent fraying or raveling (see Seam Finishes, page 64).

Fraying

With no stretch, these fabrics can be used for blouses, dresses, pants, and skirts. Some of the most common woven fabrics and their uses and characteristics are listed here. All of these can be used to make the garments in this book!

A. CHIFFON

A very lightweight, translucent fabric often used for blouses because of its beautiful drape. It's very delicate and slips easily, so use lots of pins to hold it in place when sewing! It is usually made of silk or polyester.

B. LAWN

A light- to midweight fabric with a soft texture, usually made from cotton. It's crisp but also has good drape. Some light-colored lawn can be see-through or sheer. It can be a solid color or printed with a pattern.

C. VOILE

Voile is like a mix of chiffon and lawn. It has great drape and is lightweight, soft, and breathable. It can be somewhat see-through or semi-sheer.

D. CHALLIS

Challis comes in a variety of different fibers and has a semifluid flow. Rayon challis has amazing drape, so it's frequently found in dresses and blouses. Challis has a soft surface with slight sheen and is light- to medium-weight.

E. CREPE/CREPE DE CHINE

Crepe is very similar to challis but with a textured surface. It's uber-soft and has incredible drape. It comes in a variety of thicknesses and fibers such as wool or silk.

F. LACE

Pretty and dainty, lace comes in an assortment of patterns. It's very light- to medium-weight. Lace can create girly dresses or tops.

G. CHAMBRAY

Chambray is lightweight and is commonly found in button-up shirts. It's great for spring and summer in both tops and bottoms.

H. FLANNEL

Exactly as the name says, flannel is what your favorite button-up flannel is made of. It's soft and cozy cotton or wool with a brushed texture and can be solid, printed with a pattern, or woven in a plaid pattern. Lighter flannels are used for shirts, while medium- to heavyweight flannels can be used for bottoms.

I. EYELET

Eyelet is heavily embroidered cotton fabric with small cutouts. Flowers, scallops, and curvy designs can be found on eyelet fabric. It's great for dresses, blouses, and fuller skirts. Eyelet is light- to medium-weight.

J. POPLIN

Poplin is a medium-weight fabric made from cotton or poly blends, with wrinkle resistance and easy care instructions. Sometimes it'll have a bit of spandex, which will cause the fabric to have a little stretch that is perfect for form-fitted clothing that needs to mold around your body; the stretch is helpful when going around curves.

K. SATIN

Satin has a sheen to it, so it's mostly found in special-occasion garments. It looks a lot like silk and can be made from silk—but even made from polyester it looks beautiful. Satin comes in different weights.

L. WOOL

Wool is a fiber and a very luxurious fabric that can be either incredibly soft or annoyingly scratchy, so watch out! Wool is tightly woven together to create a very dense, warm fabric. It has a brushed texture and is available from medium- to heavyweight.

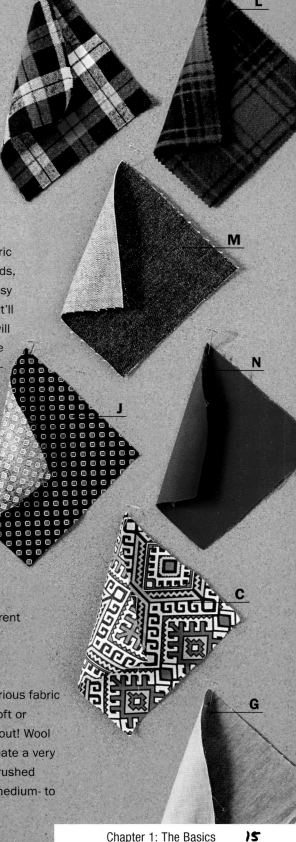

M. DENIM

Most commonly found in jeans, denim is best used for jackets or bottoms because of its sturdiness. With a little spandex, it'll also work for form-fitted items, such as super-skinny jeans. It ranges from lightweight to very heavy and thick.

N. TWILL

Twill is a light- to heavy-weight woven cotton fabric with a **diagonal weave**, which means the threads on the right side look like they run on the diagonal. It's great for apparel that requires some body, like pants or jackets.

QUILTING COTTON

Many fabric stores carry "quilting cottons" or "calico prints." Even though they come in so many fun prints and colors, they're not suited for garments. It's tempting, I know—this was all I used when I first started making my own clothes. But they don't have the drape and flow most apparel fabrics have. The clothes I made turned out stiff, and although they weren't completely unwearable, they looked awkward when worn.

KNITS

Knit fabrics, also known as "knits," are the fabrics with stretch. This is just a general rule. They're made the exact way sweaters are made—loops of yarns knitted together to create fabric—only this time, the yarn is very thin. Knits stretch, so clothes made from them don't usually need closures (zippers, buttons, etc); the fabric can be stretched to allow the garment to be put on and taken off.

Knit garments and woven garments are drafted and designed differently, since knits stretch and wovens do not. Also, knits don't ravel (the threads don't unweave themselves) unlike wovens, which always have threads on the verge of coming undone.

Knit fabrics are found in everyday wear such as T-shirts, sweaters, skirts, dresses, and even pants. Here are a couple that are frequently used and mentioned in this book.

O. JERSEY

Jersey is what T-shirts are made of; it's super comfortable to wear. Jersey is a very broad category of knit, since it describes everything from cotton jersey to wool jersey to burnout jersey. The "right" side of the fabric (the side that is shown on the outside of a garment) has the interlocking loops, while the "wrong" side (the inside of a garment) has little wavy horizontal dashes, exactly like the purl stitch in knitting. It sometimes curls at the edges when cut. Jersey comes in very light- to heavyweight.

P. DOUBLE KNIT

Double knits are thicker and sturdier than jersey. This fabric features the interlocking loops on both sides of the fabric, so there really is no right or wrong side to the fabric. "Interlock knit" is considered a double knit. Double knit is wrinkle resistant and easy to sew; it has good stretch and good stretch recovery. It comes in medium- to heavyweight. "Ponte de roma" or just "ponte" and Brazil knits also fall into this category.

Q. LACE KNIT

Like the nonstretchy version, lace knit (often simply called "stretch lace") is very pretty and feminine. The only difference is pretty obvious—lace knit stretches. It's a little harder to work with than regular lace, but the end result is so worth it. It's very lightweight.

R. THERMAL KNIT

Thermal knit is found in thermal tops and has a waffle texture. It keeps warm and is great for layering. It's lightweight.

S. SWEATER KNIT

This fabric is openly/loosely knit, just like a sweater. It's available in so many different patterns and textures/weaves. By using a sweater knit (also known as a Hacci knit), you can make a garment that looks like it was knitted when it was really sewn! How awesome is that? It comes in a variety of thicknesses.

T. SWEATSHIRT FLEECE

Sweatshirt fleece is stable and has very little stretch. It looks like a regular knit fabric on the front but has a fleece backing. Sweatshirt fleece is easy to sew but can't be used for form-fitting designs. It comes in medium- to heavyweight.

U. VELOUR

Velour is like a knit version of velvet. The wrong side looks like a regular knit fabric, and the front is soft from the cut ends of the fabric. It can be cotton or polyester. It makes great comfy clothes, like the DIY sweats (page 121).

OTHER FABRICS

The first two types of fabric below are not woven or knit. They can be used as a woven fabric, if they don't stretch. There isn't a particular grain either, because of how it's made. Many fabrics are like this, such as vinyl. Not all fabrics that are melted together are flattering (think vinyl tablecloths!), but pleather and faux suede are very wearable.

V. PLEATHER/FAUX LEATHER

Pleather looks like real leather but comes at a fraction of the cost. It's made with a plastic layer on top of a knit fabric, so some kinds have stretch. Because it's melted together, using a hot iron could melt the fabric into goopy plastic. Also, pins and needles can puncture the material and leave a permanent hole, so be careful when pinning and sewing. I suggest using low heat and a pressing cloth (a piece of scrap fabric that helps reduce the heat of the iron) on top when ironing. I also suggest using paper clips or binder clips to hold the fabric together instead of pins. You can also turn the pins so they are just in the seam allowance. Used as small details or as an entire garment, faux leather is extremely fashion-forward and chic!

W. FAUX SUEDE

Like faux leather, there's also faux suede, but it lacks stretch. It has a soft, velvety texture that feels similar to real hide. It's light- to medium-weight. Make sure you check the care instructions, as often it shouldn't be exposed to water or must be dry-cleaned.

X. SEQUINED FABRIC

With shimmer and glamour, sequined fabric is perfect for special-occasion garments. The sequins are stitched onto mesh fabric with very fine thread; when the fabric is cut, the sequins at the cut edge will fall off, and some will be cut in half. To prevent additional fallout or the sharp edges scratching you while you wear the final garment, bind all seams with bias tape (see Bias Tape, page 80).

FABRICS WITH NAP

Nap is the direction of fibers on the right side of the fabric. Some fabrics like faux fur, ultrasuede, and even corduroy, velvet, and velour have a visible nap – meaning that the fibers all point in 1 direction on the right side.

INTERFACING

Right, or non-fusible, side   Wrong, or fusible, side

Clothes often seem like they're only made out of one fabric—and the lining fabric, if applicable. But did you know that there's also a material called **interfacing** in between? Apparel that needs structure will be supported with interfacing. It's like an extra layer of fabric without the bulk. It adds strength to areas that could get worn out, such as buttonholes and waistbands. You don't usually see interfacing when it's there, because it's sandwiched between layers of fabric, but it adds body and a better grip to the fabric.

Only some clothes need interfacing, and when specified by a pattern, you have plenty of options. The kind I like to use is called **fusible interfacing**, which means it can be fused/glued to the fabric by using an iron. It's quick and easy, which is why I like it so much. Fusible interfacing comes in different weights; for most projects, I suggest using light- or medium-weight interfacing. Interfacing is sold in fabric stores by the yard, like most fabrics, and comes in black or white.

Usually the instructions for projects that require interfacing will suggest a type or weight. Always start by testing the interfacing on a scrap of the fabric you plan to use to see how it feels and to find the right setting on your iron.

To use fusible interfacing, first read over the instructions that came with the interfacing to make sure you have the correct iron settings. Place the textured side of the fusible interfacing, with the small droplets of glue facing *down,* onto the *wrong* side of the fabric. Starting with a small section, press the interfacing with an iron in an up-and-down motion. The heat from the iron melts the glue, causing the interfacing to stick to the fabric. Apply pressure for about 10–20 seconds, following the manufacturer's instructions. Then move to other sections until the entire piece of interfacing is fused to the fabric.

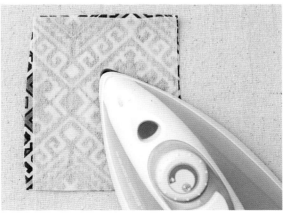

CHOOSING AND BUYING FABRIC

BUYING FABRIC IN-STORE

There is an endless supply of fabric out there and you have so many places to choose from. Your local fabric store is a great place to start. Find out if they have a mailing list or if you can get monthly discount coupons. The stores have a good selection for beginners, and the best part is that you can actually feel the fabric, so you know if you like the texture.

BUYING FABRIC ONLINE

As you get more experienced in sewing and designing, you may want to choose from a larger selection than your local fabric store carries. Another option is shopping for fabric online, where the possibilities are endless. One of my favorite websites is Fabric.com. As the name suggests, they carry a huge selection of fabric, but they also offer other crafting supplies you may need. The prices are pretty affordable, and the quality is great. I've contacted their staff quite a few times with questions about particular fabrics, and they've been happy to help. But there is a down side to online fabric shopping: you can't feel the fabric until it arrives at your house, unless the company will mail you swatches. As with any online shopping, be prepared for some surprises. I've sure had my share of those!

FINDING THE RIGHT FABRIC

Finding the perfect fabric for the clothing you're making can be a challenge, but you're sure to find something you like. When shopping, take a closer look at the project you're working on. Within every set of project instructions in this book, I've provided some suggestions of fabrics suitable for that project. The fabrics I listed will be more likely to give you a better result, but feel free to explore other options. The suggestions are just a starting point.

Before deciding on something, figure out whether you like the style of the fabric. Feel and look at the fabric. Do you like the texture? The softness? Color? Print? Is it too thick or too thin? Does it drape well? Does the weight or warmth of the fabric make sense for when and where you want to wear the garment?

Then move on to the technical questions. Is it wide enough for this project? Is there enough yardage available? Are you okay with the care instructions (especially with dry-clean-only fabrics)? The price?

When in doubt, refer to the bolt end info and go with your best judgment. If everything's okay, then you've found the perfect fabric for your project!

PREWASHING FABRIC

Have you ever washed a new shirt, only to have it shrink two sizes? It's most likely because the fabric wasn't washed before it was made into a garment. Since you're taking the time and effort to make your own clothes, you want to make sure the finished project won't shrink when washed and have all of your work go down the drain.

The best way to prevent this is to prewash your fabric. For woven fabric, first finish the cut edges by trimming with pinking shears or zigzag stitching (page 65). Then wash the entire piece of uncut fabric, following not only the fabric care label but also how you intend to wash the garment when it's finished. Then hang or lay it flat to dry, or tumble dry in the dryer, following the instructions on the fabric care label.

For most fabrics, this should be enough. However, with fabrics such as denim, where the dye may bleed, you might want to wash it a couple more times to get rid of the extra dye. Or you can use a color catcher, so it won't bleed onto other clothes and ruin them. Some rayon fabrics tend to shrink even after the first wash, so wash those a couple times as well.

Once the fabric is dry, iron it to remove any wrinkles and fold it back in half along the lengthwise grain, matching the selvages. It's now ready to be cut and made into clothing. This is pretty similar to how you would treat a store-bought garment: wash, dry, iron, and wear.

Notions

Besides fabric, there are some other tools that you'll need before you start sewing your own garments. A lot of these are purchase-once-only items, which means that once you buy one, you won't ever need to get another one again. Besides these tools, there are just a couple of smaller items such as thread, buttons, and markers.

BASIC SEWING SUPPLIES

You don't need much to get started. These items are considered my bare essentials for sewing. Here's a quick one-stop guide to what you'll need to purchase the next time you visit the store.

Sewing Shears

These scissors should be used for cutting fabrics *only*. Cutting paper with these will dull the blades, and you won't be able to get clean, precise cuts—so be sure to only use these on fabrics. They don't need to be fancy; any kind of scissors will work as long as they are sharp.

Paper Scissors

Have the normal pair of scissors you use at school for paper and anything else besides fabric you may need to cut.

PINS AND PINCUSHION

You'll need a good number of straight pins to start with for pinning fabric or patterns. I suggest getting a 100-pack just in case you run out or lose some (like me!). A pincushion will keep all your pins in one place. I recommend getting a magnetic one, as shown, because the magnet attracts all the pins without your having to look for them and pick them up!

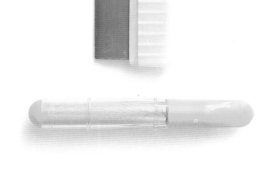

TAILOR'S CHALK

A chalk dispenser leaves a fine line of chalk behind to mark the fabric. The chalk is easily brushed away or washed out with a bit of water. My all-time favorite has to be the Chaco Liner from Clover. Not only is it easy to use, but it's also easy to replace the chalk cartridge without getting the chalk all over the place. Other chalk markers I have tried have either gone dull or are extremely messy and hard to refill. Definitely check it out!

MARKING PEN (WATER OR AIR SOLUBLE)

These special pens are great for marking fabric. The marks can be removed with a little water, or they disappear after a couple hours from the moisture in the air. I prefer these to the chalk pens, since chalk can get messy, even if you're being careful.

Water Erasable
Fabric Marking Pen

RULER

The 2″ × 18″ ruler is an absolute must for designing and drafting. The clear grid makes it easy to measure, and the marks go as small as $\frac{1}{16}$″, which give you precise measurements.

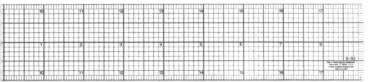

MEASURING TAPE

This is the most important measuring tool you can own. You probably already have one lying around the house. You'll use this tool to measure your body and longer lengths when the clear grid ruler isn't long enough.

HAND-SEWING NEEDLES

Keep a couple sizes on hand for different fabrics and different threads. Even if you're using a sewing machine, there are still times where hand sewing will be much easier and more precise, especially with small areas and seams.

SEAM RIPPER

Nobody's perfect and little mistakes happen, even for me! In this case, the seam ripper is your best friend! This is a tool with a tiny blade at one end used for ripping apart seams (see Seam Ripping, page 48).

SAFETY PINS

I keep a bunch of safety pins in my drawer and use them when I'm trying on a project-in-progress. Straight pins will just poke you all over the place. Ouch!

IRON AND IRONING BOARD

A good iron and ironing board will take you far. Pressing your seams with an iron is a really important step in sewing because it takes the clothes you make to a whole other level. Your iron doesn't have to be fancy; it just needs to be sturdy and have adjustable heat settings for different fabrics.

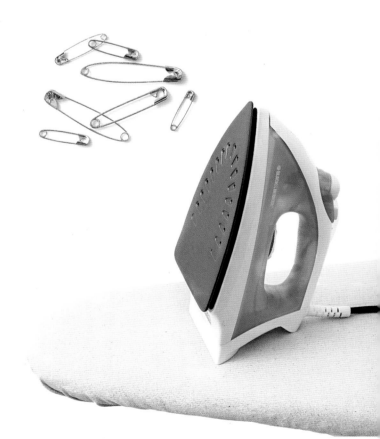

THREAD

I always have thread in neutral colors such as white and black in my stash (see More About Thread, page 26). While matching the color to your fabric is nice, these two basics are the most versatile and can go with almost any fabric. They're great to have as backups when you run out of the color you want.

TRACING PAPER/PATTERN PAPER

You might already have some of this at home or at school! I trace my patterns onto tracing paper to preserve the original. There's special paper just for patterns, but you can use tracing paper, tissue paper (like for presents), freezer paper (used for wrapping up foods to freeze, but also sold in quilt shops), or any large sheet of paper that you can see the original lines through.

SEWING MACHINE NEEDLES

If you plan to use a sewing machine, you will need to get needles for the machine. There are many different types and sizes, so check out the Sewing Machine Needles chart (page 26) to figure out which is the best for your project.

BOBBINS

These are used in a sewing machine. Make sure the kind you're using is the right type and size for your machine. Keep a couple on hand.

ADDITIONAL ITEMS

These items aren't essentials needed for sewing, but they're nice to have and can come in handy.

PAINTER'S TAPE

This tape is used for marking straight lines, taping things together, and marking pieces of fabric. Painter's tape is much easier to peel off compared to other tapes, and it comes in a variety of widths.

SMALL SCISSORS

Smaller scissors are so useful when trimming threads or cutting small pieces. They can make small cuts and work in tight places where normal shears can't reach.

HOOKS AND EYES

These are completely optional but are great for holding the uppermost edge of a garment closed, such as where the zipper doesn't quite reach at the top of your dress or the small gap where the waistband of the shorts meets above the zipper.

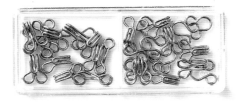

ZIPPERS

Zippers come in all different colors, weights, materials, and lengths and add a fun little finishing touch. There are different types of zippers for different types of garments and accessories.

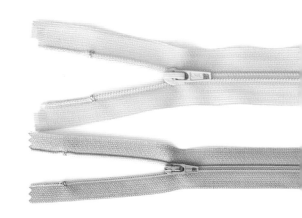

ELASTIC

Elastic is commonly used in garment sewing to gather while allowing some stretch. It's nice to have a variety of widths in your stash.

MORE ABOUT THREAD

Since thread holds clothes together, it plays a very important role in garment construction. Keep in mind the thread's color and content, as well as your intended project.

I use an all-purpose polyester sewing thread for garment sewing. Yes, I use polyester. You might think to use cotton thread to sew garments out of cotton fabric. But even though cotton thread is good for quilts and home decor, it doesn't have the "give" and strength that clothes need when they are put on our bodies. The thread may snap or break when the garment is being put on or stretched as we move.

You can use a topstitching thread for a decorative touch on heavyweight fabrics (like for the shorts or pants) or a fine thread for extra-lightweight fabrics.

Picking a thread color that's similar to the fabric is a common choice, but contrasting thread can be used for decorative touches where you want the stitching to stand out. I personally just like to stick with neutral colors such as black, white, cream, and gray, just so I can sew multiple garments at once without worrying about thread color.

MORE ABOUT SEWING MACHINE NEEDLES

NEEDLE SIZE

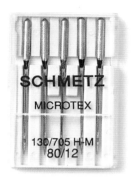

Sewing machine needles come in different types and sizes. They're usually sold in packages of five in a small case. The needle size is represented with two numbers. The first number is the needle's metric size (i.e. 75 is a .75 mm diameter), and the second number is its U.S. standard size. It doesn't matter which number you look at: the smaller the number, the finer the needle; the bigger the number, the larger the needle. Always choose a needle according to your fabric weight to prevent any puckering or holes.

Sewing Machine Needles

FABRIC WEIGHT	EXAMPLES	NEEDLE SIZE
Very light	Chiffon, lawn	70/10
Light	Voile, crepe, lace, lawn	80/12
Medium	Flannel, eyelet, poplin, satin, wool, pleather/ faux leather, suede	80/12 or 90/14
Heavy	Wool, pleather, denim, twill	90/14 or 100/16
Very heavy	Wool, denim, twill	100/16
Knits	All knits	80/12

Needle Types

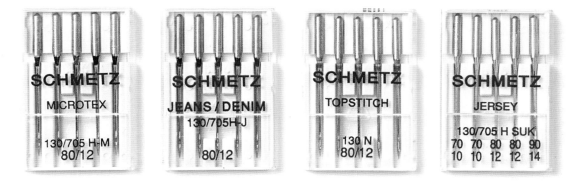

Microtex needles are my favorites to use on woven fabrics because of their really sharp points that can pierce through the threads. Use on finely woven fabrics.

Denim needles also work great on heavier woven fabrics because of their nice pointed tips and strength. They go through woven fabrics easily for easy stitching, so use them on all sorts of woven fabrics.

Topstitching needles are used for decorative stitching with a thick thread, like the stitching found on jeans. These needles have a larger hole for the thread to pass through and are able to pierce through many layers of fabric.

Ballpoint/jersey or stretch needles are used for knits because they have a rounded tip that can slip between the knit loops of the fabric without actually piercing or cutting the loops, which could cause holes. Use stretch needles for fabric with a high spandex (page 13) content.

There's also a very common needle called the **universal needle**. Some people think that this needle works fine, but it can actually cause disasters. See, universal needles are supposed to be woven- *and* knit-fabric safe. But the problem is that because the needle needs to accommodate two very different fabrics, it needs to be sharp yet not sharp at the same time. The result is a neither sharp nor round needle. It doesn't glide through wovens because it's not pointy enough, yet it snags the yarns on knits because it's not completely rounded. Use a woven fabric needle (microtex, denim, or topstitching) for wovens and a ballpoint needle for knits. End of story.

After a period of usage, needles can get dull, just like pencils do. It's best to change them every 6–8 hours or so of sewing. By 6–8 hours, I mean 6–8 hours straight of stitching. This means that ironing or cutting or any time in between using the machine doesn't count. Therefore, your needles may last a little longer than you expect. When the stitching starts to seem a little off, rethread the upper thread and bobbin thread and be sure to try a new needle as well.

Sewing by Hand and Machine

You have two options when it comes it sewing: by hand or by sewing machine. While all of the projects in this book can be sewn by hand, they can be sewn a lot faster if you use a sewing machine.

SEWING MACHINE

Tips on Buying a Sewing Machine

If you're in the market for getting a sewing machine, I have a couple of tips and things to look for that will hopefully help. There are many brands and types out there, so it's easy to get overwhelmed.

- Get a machine with a powerful motor, not something flimsy. You want a quality machine that will sew through many layers of fabric.

- A simple but sturdy machine is the best. There's no need for any fancy stitching if you're just starting out.

- Look for a machine that converts to a free arm for easier sewing-in-the-round.

- Find a machine with a horizontal drop-in bobbin. This kind is much easier to put in rather than fiddling with a vertical bobbin. Plus you can easily see if the bobbin thread is low.

- Look for an adjustable stitch length. This allows you to adjust the length of the stitches, which is incredibly useful.

- Consider what accessories the machine comes with.

- Buy from a local dealer, not a big-box or fabric chain store. The quality is usually much better, you can try out the machine, and the dealer may have some basic how-to classes to teach you how to use and clean your machine. The dealership is likely to service machines too, so you're gaining a warranty with them. In addition, if your machine starts acting weird, you can take it to them to figure out your problem, unlike big chain stores that cannot do anything to help you.

- Always try out the machine. Ask yourself, is this what I want to be working with? Is it running smoothly? Does the noise bother me? How is the stitching quality? Do I like where the functions and buttons are?

- Find something you can grow into but not something so big that it's crazy intimidating.

My favorite brand of sewing machine is Babylock. Babylock makes quality machines that will last and are super user friendly.

Sewing Machine Anatomy

All sewing machines are made and will function differently. While I can't give you a full tutorial on how to use yours, I can give you the basic anatomy of the parts of the machine. I highly suggest you read your sewing machine user's manual to learn all the details of your machine.

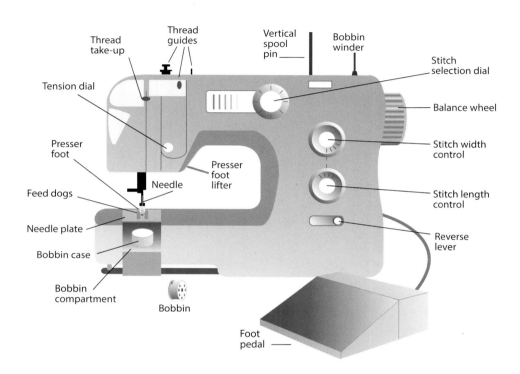

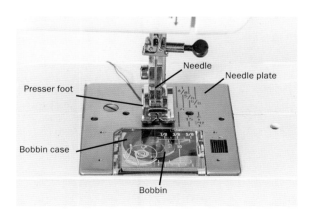

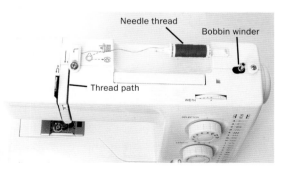

TYPES OF STITCHES

Many machines come with a variety of stitches, but only a few are essential to sewing garments.

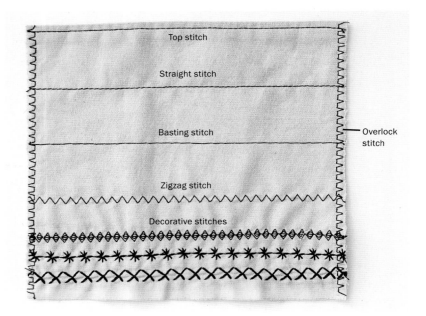

STRAIGHT STITCH

This is the most basic stitch that you'll be using all the time. It can't be used for all seams, but if the instructions don't say what stitch to use, just use this one.

BASTING STITCH

A basting stitch is the same setting as the straight stitch but longer in length. It's used for temporarily sewing two pieces together without fussing with pins. The larger stitches help you pull out the threads when you no longer need them. Just set the straight stitch to the longest stitch length it can go to. This stitch is also used to make gathers (page 78).

TOP STITCH

This stitch is very similar to the straight stitch; it's just used decoratively. You'll see the stitching on the outside of the garment, so sew as neatly as possible. Use a normal stitch length and sew close to the fold or seam you're topstitching on.

ZIGZAG STITCH

This stitch is used for knit fabrics because it has more elasticity and "give" to it. It's also used to finish off raw edges (see Zigzag Stitch Seam Finish, page 65).

OVERLOCK STITCH

The overlock stitch is a type of zigzag stitch that wraps around the edge of the fabric and is similar to the serged seam seen on the inside of store-bought garments. It's used to finish off raw edges.

DECORATIVE STITCHES

These fun little patterned stitches can be used to embellish your sewing by adding a subtle but intricate detail. I love these on hems in a contrasting color to mimic hand embroidery.

HAND SEWING

Even if you plan on machine sewing your garments, you'll still be sewing small details by hand. Hand sewing gives you so much more control over your project. Although it takes time, it can produce incredible results. Always use a double strand of thread (looped through the eye of the needle, folded in half, and knotted at the other end) to create secure stitches.

Types of Stitches

RUNNING STITCH

This is the hand version of the straight stitch. Go in and out of the fabric and pull the thread through to create the running stitch. For a hand-basting stitch, just poke the needle in and out at larger intervals.

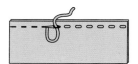

BACKSTITCH

This is a very strong stitch. I suggest using this stitch rather than the running stitch for sewing seams because it's a lot more secure. Bring the needle out of the fabric and take a stitch backward; then bring the needle up a half-stitch in front, and then take another stitch backward. Repeat to sew the seam.

WHIPSTITCH

The whipstitch makes a very narrow seam and is suitable for attaching lace to the edge of a garment. Bring the needle from the back to the front. Continue to do this, creating loops over the edges of the fabric.

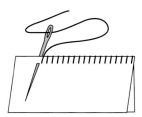

SLIP STITCH

A slip stitch joins two pieces along their folds. It's a very delicate and almost undetectable stitch used for closing gaps or creating an invisible hem. Sew a tiny stitch through one layer of the fabric, catching only a couple threads. Bring the needle to the other side and sew a tiny stitch there, catching only a couple threads. Repeat.

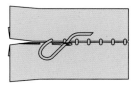

Seam Allowance

You probably already know what a **seam** is: it's the stitching that holds 2 pieces of fabric together. The **seam allowance** is how far the stitching is from the raw edge of the fabric inside the garment.

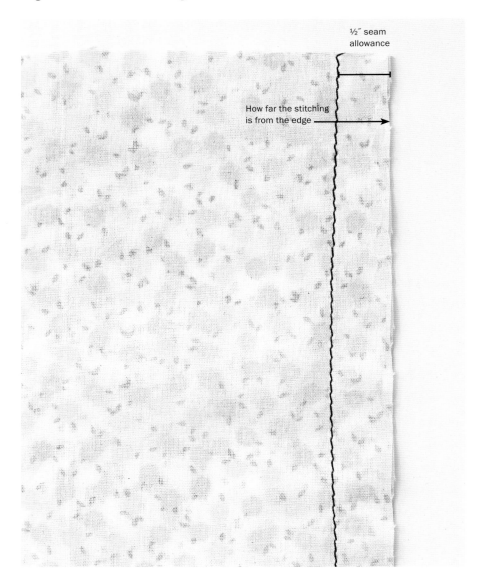

½" seam allowance

How far the stitching is from the edge

So, when I say "sew a ½˝ seam" or "use a ½˝ seam allowance," I really mean to sew a line of stitching ½˝ away from the edge(s) of the fabric. This measurement may change according to the projects in the book, but the concept is the same.

It's important to follow the seam allowance specified in the project instructions because the pattern was drafted for this measurement. These extra inches were built into the pattern for you to sew the seam.

Many commercial garment patterns tell you to sew with a ⅝˝ seam allowance. Always check what the pattern pieces and instructions say, and then follow that at your sewing machine.

The patterns in this book were drafted using a ½˝ seam allowance. In some special places (like attaching the neckbands), I will tell you to sew with a ¼˝ seam allowance.

If you were to use a different seam allowance than specified, you could end up with a different-sized garment. For example, if a top was supposed to be made with a ½˝ seam allowance, but you used a 1˝ seam allowance instead, then you made the top an extra ½˝ smaller on all sides. A top is made out of a front and back piece, and both have two side seam edges, which totals to four side seam edges. Multiply that by ½˝, and you've got 2˝. That's making the top a whole size smaller! See how a seam allowance change of as little as ½˝ could affect the entire sizing of the garment?

It's not hard at all to sew with a seam allowance, ½˝ or otherwise. Most sewing machines have a handy little guide built into the metal plate under the presser foot and needle. Find the specified measurement on the plate and line up the fabric edge(s) against this line. Now all you have to do is make sure the edges are lining up with this line as you sew your seam.

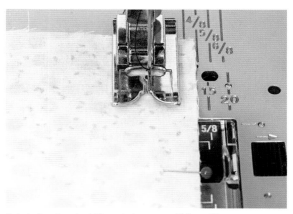

Fabric lined up to ½˝ mark (same as ⁴⁄₈˝ mark)

Another option is to place your clear gridded ruler underneath the needle and measure the seam allowance away to the right of the needle. In the picture below, I'm measuring ¼˝ away for a ¼˝ seam allowance. Then I'm lining up the edge of a piece of painter's tape against the ruler where I've marked out ¼˝ and pressing firmly to secure the tape. When sewing a seam, I'll just line up my fabric with the line of the tape. Easy, right?

SEWING A SEAM

Seams are essential to garments (duh), so it's good to practice sewing seams and to fully understand how seams are sewn and how they work.

NOTE

The **right side** of the fabric is the side you want on the outside of your garment, while the **wrong side** is the side of the fabric that's going to be on the inside.

Right or "pretty" side

Wrong side

1 Place 2 pieces of fabric right sides together, meaning the pretty sides of the fabric are facing in while the wrong sides are facing out. You do this so the finished seam is on the inside of the garment when worn and unseen from the outside. A lot of instructions will say to sew a seam right sides together; if it's not written, it's automatically assumed. Just place the pieces on top of each other and line up the edges.

2 Pin the pieces along the edges where the seam is going to be sewn (see Pinning, page 47).

3 Sew a straight line (or zigzag stitch, page 30, depending on the instructions) down the edges, using the specified seam allowance. Always backstitch (sew in reverse) at the start and end of every seam to create a knot. Machines can't tie a knot, so backstitching is used to ensure that the seam won't come apart. You can usually do this by pressing a button or knob on your sewing machine that has the reverse sign on it. Some machines have a lockstitch feature that is like a knot, so check your manual. Pull the fabric out of the machine and cut the top and bobbin threads close to the stitching.

4 Open up the pieces so the right sides of the fabric are now facing up. Press it flat. You've now sewn a seam!

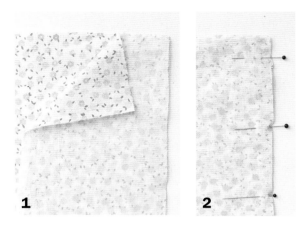

1

2

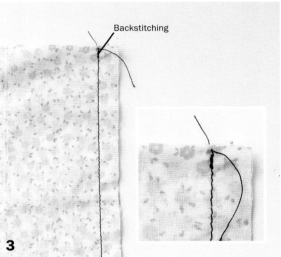

Backstitching

3

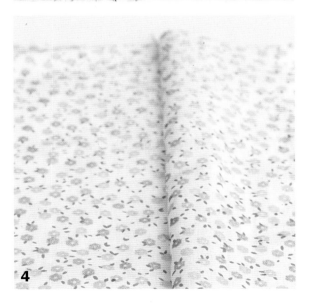

4

DIY Infinity Scarf

If you asked whether I prefer a traditional scarf or an infinity scarf, I would most definitely say the infinity scarf. They're so easy to style without having to mess with the ends or trying to find the perfect length, making it the ideal accessory for every season. And, it just so happens, they're super easy to make! Infinity scarves can be pricey, but by making your own, you can choose the print and customize them to your style for cheap. Once you get the hang of it, these are great gifts, since they take under 30 minutes to make!

FABRIC SUGGESTIONS

Any kind of fabric, both knits and wovens, will work for this scarf. From cotton lawn to wools to shiny satins to sweater knits: as long as the fabric is at least 60˝ wide, you can use whatever your heart desires! Since the design is pretty simple, the fabric you choose to work with will really have a big impact on the finished project. Light-and-breezy fabrics such as voile are perfect for spring scarves, while thick knits are great for fall and winter. Lace will make a beautiful and delicate scarf, while a medium-weight knit could be used to make an everyday scarf. Use what you've learned about fabrics so far to pick out the ideal fabric for this project!

SUPPLIES

- 1 yard of 60˝-wide fabric
- Thread to match your fabric
- Basic sewing supplies

SKILLS CHECKLIST

The Basics (Chapter 1, page 9)

Basic Techniques (Chapter 2):

- Pinning (page 47)
- Pressing Seams (page 49)

Your creativity, style, and determination!

CUTTING

The 1-yard cut of fabric is already the perfect size for this project. There's no need to cut it smaller. Just prewash your fabric before continuing, and you should be good to go!

SEWING

Use a ½˝ seam allowance, unless otherwise noted.

Note: In the following photographs, the models were made at a smaller scale and sewn in contrasting thread for demonstration purposes.

1 Fold the fabric in half lengthwise, right sides together, lining up the long raw edges. This forms a long tube that should measure approximately 18˝ × 60˝. Pin the raw edges together.

2 Sew down the pinned edge.

3 Turn the tube inside out, so the right side of the fabric is now outside.

2

4 Shift the seam, so it's now running down the center of the tube. Give the seam a light press. Don't press too hard, or the scarf will flatten. Just run the iron over the seam quickly and lightly.

5 Bring the 2 ends of the scarf together, forming a loop. Make sure the loop isn't twisted.

6 On 1 end, fold ½˝ over to the wrong side all around the tube. Press to make a crease.

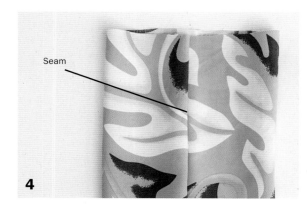

Seam

4

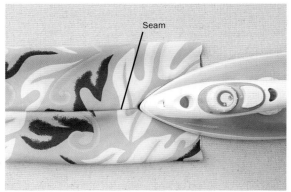

Seam

6

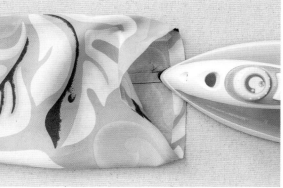

7 Place the other end of the tube inside the folded end, covering the raw edges. Pin down the width of the tube.

8 Sew ¼˝ away from the fold through all the layers, or as close as you can get, to join the ends. And that's it! Loop it twice around your neck to wear.

7

8

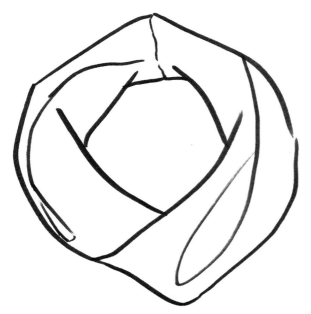

CHAPTER 2

THE DETAILS THAT MATTER

Are you having fun yet? Getting a solid foundation is important with any hobby, sewing and designing included. That is why you'll learn about some techniques commonly used as you sew so you can really master them. I'll also introduce you to patterns, which you copy and use to cut out specific shapes of fabric to sew together to make a garment. Combining what you've learned about fabrics, seam allowances, and stitches from Chapter 1 (page 9), you'll be ready to tackle an actual clothing item (the really cute DIY Basic Tee, page 60) as your second project!

Patterns

A **sewing pattern** is like a guide for how big and in what shape to cut your fabric. You use those guides to create paper **patterns**, which are used to cut out pieces of fabric that will be sewn to create a three-dimensional item that fits the human body. A garment has many parts (sleeves, back, front, and so on), so there will be a pattern piece for each part that you'll copy and use to cut your fabric. Sometimes I will tell you to cut a rectangle at a certain size; in that case, you can use your ruler to make your own paper pattern or mark the shape directly on the fabric.

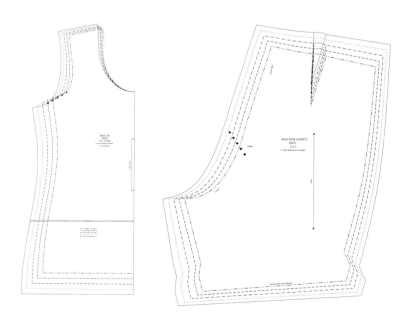

TRACING PATTERNS

All the projects in this book have patterns (with the exception of the DIY Infinity Scarf, page 36) and are printed on the pattern pullout pages at the back of this book. Each project will tell you which pattern pullout page contains the pattern pieces you will need.

The sheets are printed on both sides, so you can't just cut into the paper without ruining the patterns on the back. You also want to keep each pattern in all of its sizes, so you can make clothes in different sizes—whether it's because you're growing or you're making something for a friend who's not the same size as you. Therefore, you will need to trace onto paper each pattern you need in the correct size. There's no need to trace every single pattern; just trace the ones you need for the garment you want to make.

Just like shopping in stores, where every brand or designer has slightly different sizes, my designs are offered in different sizes. Measure yourself to see what size fits you best—don't just assume you know what you size you will be.

1 Measure your body and figure out your size using the chart at right.

Since most of the patterns have stretch or are roomy, if your measurements are slightly different from what is listed on the chart, they should still fit.

If you're making a top, use the bust and waist measurements. If you're making a skirt or shorts, use your hip and waist measurements. If you're between sizes, use the larger size; you can always take the garment in, but you can't make it bigger.

Each pattern piece has multiple lines. These lines represent the different sizes of the garment. Each line makes a different sized garment. The different sizes are differentiated by different styles of lines.

	EXTRA-SMALL	SMALL	MEDIUM	LARGE	EXTRA-LARGE
Bust	28″	30″	32″	34″	36″
Waist	24″	24″	25½″	27″	28½″
Hips	30″	32″	34″	36″	38″

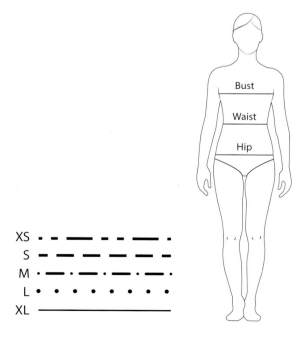

XS · — · — · — · — · — ·
S — — — — — —
M · — · — · — · — ·
L · · · · · · · ·
XL ———————————

2 Find the pattern pieces for the garment you want to make.

Each pattern is labeled with the project name on it, and the project instructions tell you how many pieces there are for that garment. Find the style of line that corresponds with your size. This is the line you'll be following the entire time you're using the patterns from this book—unless you change sizes.

3 Lay a large sheet of paper on top of the pattern pieces. I like to use tracing paper, which can be found in inexpensive rolls at the craft or art store.

4 Create templates by tracing along the lines that correspond to your size. Be sure to also trace any markings (the triangles, lines, arrows) and label the piece with the information listed on the pattern, such as the name, seam allowance, and what piece of the garment it is (front, back, and so on).

5 Repeat Steps 2–4 for all the other pattern pieces that belong to the project you're working on.

6 Cut out your paper patterns. You'll be cutting right on the line later, so you don't need to be exact now. If you're concerned about using your fabric scissors to cut through tracing paper, however, certainly cut the pattern right on the line now.

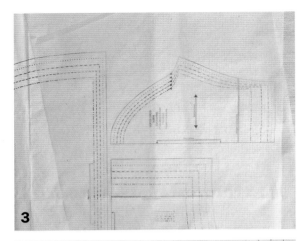

3

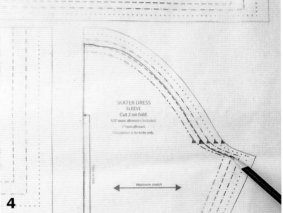

4

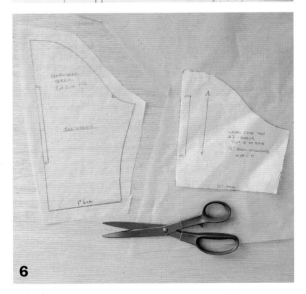

6

PATTERN SYMBOLS

It's time to demystify all those weird lines and symbols you traced! If you forgot to do that, just lay your pattern back on top of the sheets and trace those markings.

GRAINLINE ARROW

This arrow needs to be parallel to the selvages when you pin your pattern to the fabric. If it is crooked, the garment will hang funny when it is finished.

Grain

PLACE-ON-FOLD ARROW

This double-sided arrow indicates that the edge that it's pointing to needs to be placed on a fold of fabric. The pattern only represents half of the fabric piece. For your pattern to be cut at full size, it needs to be placed on a folded edge of fabric so that when you open up the fabric, it's one full-size, symmetrical piece.

Place on fold.

DARTS

These weird little triangles help shape flat fabric to go around a three-dimensional curve. You'll learn more about darts in Chapter 4 (page 75).

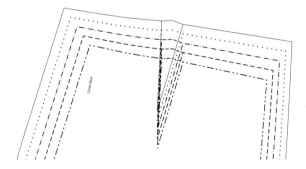

NOTCHES

Notches are the small triangles or perpendicular lines at the edge of the pattern. Cut the shape outside the seam allowance when cutting out the pattern. Notches act as a guide to which pieces should be matched up where. When two pieces need to be sewn together, the notches should be matched together before you continue to pin the rest of the seam.

LENGTHEN OR SHORTEN LINE

This is where you'd alter the pattern to make the finished garment longer or shorter. See Lengthening and Shortening (page 92) for more info.

Lengthen or shorten here.

CUTTING LAYOUTS

Cutting layouts are the diagrams that show you how to lay out your patterns onto your fabric. The way shown is probably the most efficient use of the fabric. You can lay the pattern pieces out differently, but keep in mind that you might need more fabric to accommodate them.

Some patterns will give different layouts for "w/ nap" or "w/o nap." That means if you use a fabric with nap (page 19), you will need to lay out all the pattern pieces with the top in the same direction. You'll need to do this if you have a fabric with a printed design that has a definite direction, too.

For all the cutting layouts shown in the book, assume the layout is for a fabric with nap.

Just fold your fabrics according to the diagram and place your pattern pieces on top. Make sure the grainline is parallel to the selvages.

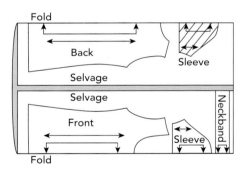

Fabric right side

Fabric wrong side

Pattern wrong (unmarked) side; sometimes the pattern pieces fit better if they are placed right side down.

CUTTING AND MARKING FABRIC

Once your patterns are all laid flat, pin them to the fabric. Don't use too many pins; otherwise, you'll get ripples.

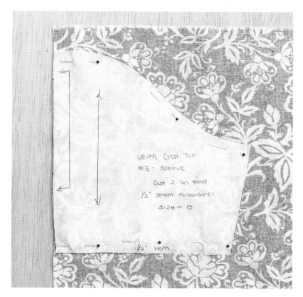

Then use your fabric scissors to cut around them like you did when cutting out your pattern.

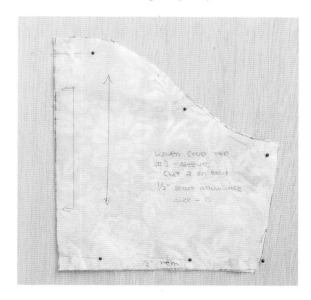

Before removing your pattern from the fabric, you need to transfer some markings from your pattern to the fabric. You only need to transfer the notches and darts, if applicable. If there aren't any, feel free to move on.

TRANSFERRING NOTCHES

Cut a little triangle on the edge exactly like the marking shows. If you're working with two layers of fabric, make sure both pieces are marked.

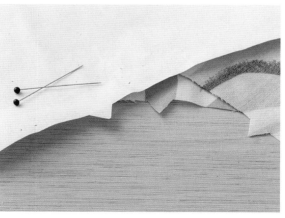

Marking Darts

If your patterns are on sturdy paper, use this easy way to mark the darts: Cut out the entire triangle shape and draw along the cutout using chalk or a marking pen on the *wrong* side of the fabric. Flip the pattern over to the other half of the fabric piece (the other side of the fold) and trace the cutout on that half as well so that it's mirrored.

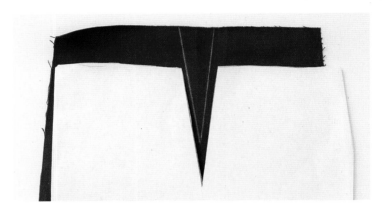

If you traced your patterns onto a lightweight paper like tissue paper, cutting out the dart may make your pattern tear when you use it again.

Use a removable fabric marker to mark the two ends of the dart at the edge of the fabric on the wrong side.

Push a straight pin through the point of the dart, lift the pattern paper up, and mark that point as well.

When you unpin the pattern piece, draw the dart by using a ruler to connect the three marks.

And that's all for patterns! Unpin them from the fabric pieces and move onto sewing. Yay!

Basic Techniques

These are a couple of basic techniques that I frequently use when sewing. Not every single sewing technique is listed here—just the ones that will be used in almost every project in this book. These will take you, as a beginner, far. I suggest practicing on scrap fabric before working on a project to really get the hang of the techniques.

PINNING

Pinning is as easy as it sounds! Insert pins about 1˝–2˝ apart perpendicular to the seam that you're sewing, as shown. That way, you'll be able to pull them out from the right as you sew. Remember to take the pins out before they get to the needle or they may snap into pieces and fly into your face! This happened to me once and, boy, did I learn my lesson!

MEASURING AND MARKING

You probably do this very simple technique often in school. Measuring and marking is the same on fabric as it is on paper. Just follow the directed measurements and use the gridded ruler to measure out points. Mark the points using tailor's chalk or a marking pen. Test the chalk or pen on the fabric beforehand to make sure you can remove it; always mark on the wrong side of the fabric, so if any markings can't be removed, they'll end up on the inside of the garment.

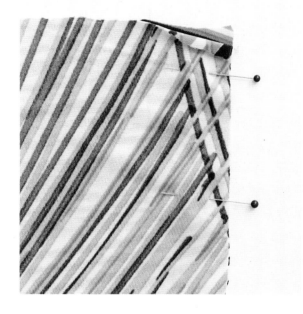

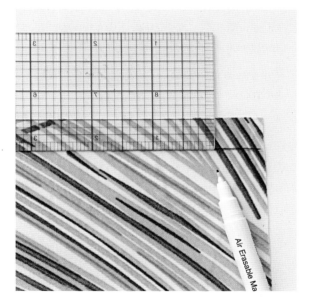

SEAM RIPPING

Everyone makes mistakes, including me. That's what a seam ripper is for! The seam ripper helps you pick out stitches quickly and easily. The end of the seam ripper comes with two little points. The longer and sharper end is the blade, and the rounded end is to prevent you from cutting the fabric with the blade.

To rip out a seam, insert the blade into a stitch and slide the thread all the way down the shaft to where the two ends meet and where the blade is. The thread should break. You don't have to rip out every single stitch, just rip every three stitches or so. Then pull the two pieces of fabric apart and the seam should come apart.

PRESSING SEAMS

As I think we all know, a wrinkled shirt is simply no fun, which makes ironing a necessity. That's the kind of ironing you do for finished clothes. But when you're sewing clothes, ironing is also called "pressing," as in pressing a seam by using the iron. So, whenever I say "press this" or "give it a press" in this book, I really mean to iron the seam so there are no wrinkles or weird folds. Use the right setting on the iron for the fabric's fiber content to avoid burning the fabric or having to press forever for a crease to disappear.

First, press the seam as you stitched it with both layers together and wrong sides out.

Then open up the fabric and press the seam allowances again, either as directed in the instructions or following these general guidelines:

- **Side, center front, and center back seams:** Press the seam allowances open (so there is one seam allowance on either side of the seam).

- **Sleeve seams:** Press toward the sleeve.

- **Dart:** Press down (bust) or to the center (waist).

For most other seams, press down or to the back.

Pressing the seams as you sew them will really make a difference, trust me. It'll give you a more professional finish and a store-bought look.

SEWING CURVED SEAMS

Curved seams are common in garment construction because our bodies aren't rectangles or sticks! Curved seams are needed when sewing together two curved pieces of fabric; they also help shape it to fit our bodies. There's no trick to sewing curved seams—just carefully maneuver the fabric with your hands, making sure the seam allowances stay lined up and stay the correct size. Sew a little more slowly, gradually turning the fabrics. When you need to move more to follow the curve, stop with the needle down in the fabric, lift up the presser foot to adjust the fabric, and then put the foot back down and continue sewing.

SEWING IN THE ROUND

Sometime the seam you're sewing isn't in a straight line: it's in a circle, like on waistlines or armholes. It may seem pretty confusing, but it's as easy as sewing in a straight line.

1 Insert 1 piece into the other, right sides together. Pin the pieces together at the edges, starting at any seams that need to be matched and continuing around in a circle until you reach where you started.

2 Slide the pinned garment into the sewing machine. It doesn't matter where you start sewing, just pick a point and start stitching. Remember to backstitch at the beginning!

3 Keep on going until you reach where you started. Since the fabric is in a tube, you'll go around full circle until you see the start of the stitching. Make sure there are no wrinkles or weird folds as you sew.

4 Sew a couple of stitches to overlap the starting point. Backstitch and cut your threads.

1

2

3

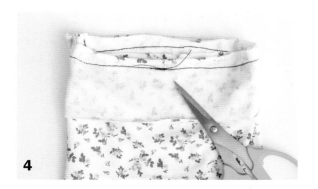

4

HEMMING

Hems are used to finish off the bottom edge on garments. The measurements used in the following examples may differ from the projects. You're free to use whatever sized hem you think looks the most flattering on you.

Single Turned Hem

Fold ½˝ of fabric to the wrong side of the fabric, pinning as needed. Press the fold. Work around the entire edge until there aren't any raw edges visible on the right side. Sew close to the raw edge using a straight stitch. This hem is okay for knits that won't fray, but it will not work for woven fabrics.

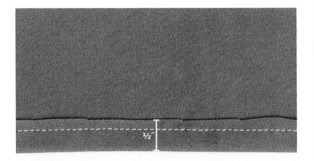 

Double Turned Hem

Fold ¼˝ of fabric to the wrong side of the fabric, pinning as needed. Press the fold. Fold ¼˝ again, hiding all the raw edges. Press. Stitch close to the inner fold using a medium-length straight stitch. This is a good way to hem wovens.

 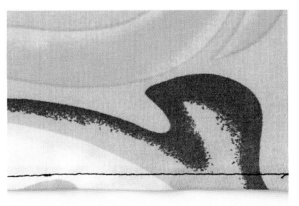

CASINGS—THREADING ELASTIC

A casing is a stitched tunnel all around the edge of a garment, like a sleeve, waistband, or pant hem. Inside it will have a piece of elastic for a stretchy comfortable fit.

Here's how to make a casing and add elastic.

1 Fold ¼˝ to the wrong side of the fabric. Press.

2 Fold the edge again to the wrong side. Use the width of your elastic plus ¼˝ to determine how much. For example, ½˝ elastic + ¼˝ = ¾˝. Press.

3 Sew close to the inner fold, around the entire waistline, in the round (page 50). Leave a 1˝ gap unsewn. This is the casing for the elastic.

4 Cut a piece of elastic that's long enough to go around your waist. Add a safety pin to one end. Use the gap you left open to thread the elastic through the casing. Push the safety pin to pull the elastic.

1

2

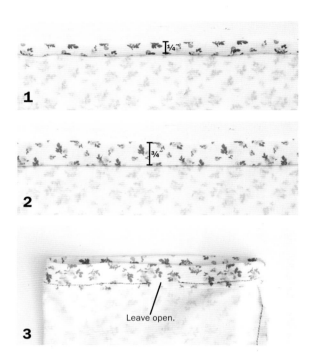

Leave open.

3

4

5 Continue pushing the safety pin until it comes out the other end of the gap in the casing. Overlap the 2 elastic ends. Safety pin them together and try on the garment for fit.

6 Adjust the ends of the elastic if you need them tighter or looser. Then sew them together using a straight or a zigzag stitch, going over the area multiple times to make sure it's secure.

7 Switch back to straight stitch and sew the gap of the casing closed to finish the waistband.

SEWING WITH KNITS

Unlike woven fabrics, knits are stretchy, so the seams need to be stretchy too. When sewing with knits, just replace the normal straight stitch with a zigzag stitch, which has more flexibility and can stretch with the fabric. Some machines have a specific knit stitch setting, often 1.0 wide and 2.5 long. Also, *don't* stretch knit fabrics when you sew (see some exceptions below). Stretching knit fabrics will just create an ugly rippled seam.

STRETCH AND SEW

Despite the fact that knits shouldn't be stretched while sewing, there are a couple exceptions. One of them is when a shorter length of fabric needs to be fitted to a larger length or circumference, like a neckband, or when elastic is sewn in at the waist. The reasoning behind this is to avoid gaping. If you cut the band to be the same length as the neckline, the neckline wouldn't lie flat and would gape. By cutting it a little shorter, it cinches the neckline and helps the band lie flat. But in order for the shorter piece to fit into the larger, it needs to be stretched to fit.

Place the shorter piece on the top so it's visible. Starting at one point, gently stretch the top (shorter) layer *a little* as you sew. Use your other hand to help feed the fabric through the back. Continue the seam this way, but remember not to go overboard with the stretching.

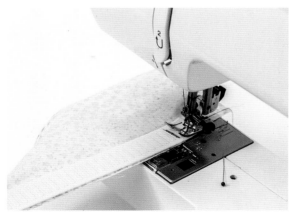

SEWING A NECKBAND

Many knit tops and dresses have a neckband along the neckline to finish off the edge. See the following instructions on how to insert one into a garment. Note that this method is only for knit fabrics, since wovens behave differently and therefore need to be treated in a different way. This is also how an elastic waistband is attached to the waistline of a skirt when the waistband is smaller than the waistline measurement.

1

2

3

1 Sew the neckband strip together along the short edges using a ½˝ seam allowance. Then fold it in half *wrong sides together*, matching up the long edges. Press.

2 Fold the neckband loop in half on the seam and then in half again. Stick a pin where the fabric is folded. You should end up with 4 pins equally spaced marking the quarters.

3 Mark 4 equal points on the neckline of the shirt/dress. Start with the center front and center back as your 2 starting points. Bring the 2 points together in the center; the 2 folds on the right and left will be the remaining 2 points. Mark them with pins.

4 With the right side of the garment facing out, match the points on the neckband to the points on the neckline. The seam on the neckband matches with the center back. You may notice the neckband is smaller than the neckline, which is perfectly normal as this helps keep the neckline of the top from stretching out over time.

5 Line up the edges of the neckband to the neckline and, using a straight stitch, sew in the round (page 50) around the entire neckline. Start from 1 point and stretch the neckband strip to fit the neckline as you sew. Stretch enough so that the band is equal in length to the neckline between the 2 marks. Work in sections (4 sections total in between the pins). The points are evenly spaced, so the amount of fabric being stretched is equal all the way around.

6 Press the neckband away from the body and the seam allowances toward the body of the garment.

SETTING IN SLEEVES

Many garments we wear have sleeves, so it only makes sense to learn how to make and attach them. I was very intimidated when I didn't know how to sew a sleeve, but it's a common sewing task that isn't as hard as many people think. Once you get the hang of it, it's as easy as sewing a regular seam. This way of adding sleeves is called "setting in the sleeve(s)."

1 Fold the sleeve pieces in half, wrong sides together, as shown. Sew the **side seam** (the straight, vertical edge) using a ½˝ seam allowance. Turn the sleeve pieces right side out.

2 With the body of the dress or top wrong side out, slide the sleeve into the armhole, so the pieces are right sides together.

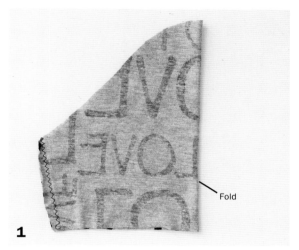

Fold

1

Zigzag stitch used for knits

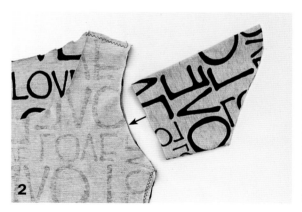

2

3 Pick up the 2 pieces together at the side seam so you're facing it as shown. Match the sleeve seam to the body side seam. Pin in place.

4 Start working your way around the circumference of the armhole, matching the raw edges of the sleeve to the edges of the garment body. Pin as you go.

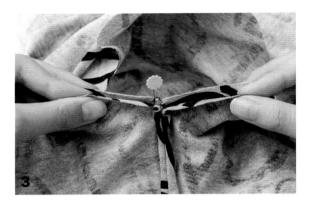

5 Sewing in the round (page 50), sew a ½˝ seam all the way around the entire armhole until you come back to your starting point. Check to make sure no extra fabric was caught in the seam. If there was, use a seam ripper to remove the stitches for that section, pin it back in place, and then try again.

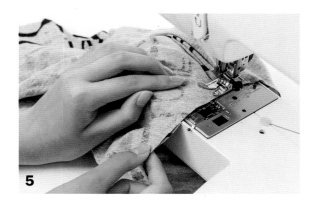

6 Repeat Steps 1–5 on the other armhole and sleeve. Turn the entire garment (sleeves attached) right side out and you're finished with your sleeves!

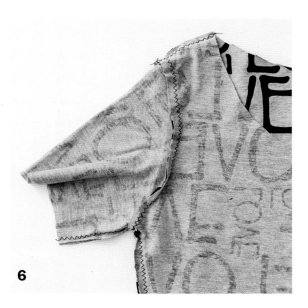

DIY Basic Tee

T-shirts are essential in anyone's wardrobe. Whether they're for layering or to throw on with jeans for a simple outfit, you can never have enough T-shirts. In fact, I bet you're wearing one right now! Now you can choose the fabric and color, making it your own! Make one, and you'll be whipping them out in an hour or less. Why not test your newfound sewing skills while you're at it?

FABRIC SUGGESTIONS

Cotton jersey is the most common choice for making a basic tee. For something more sweater-like, you could also use sweater knits or any other kind of knit. Choose something comfortable and stretchy, so you can wear this as an everyday top.

SUPPLIES

- Knit fabric, 60˝ wide:

    For sizes XS–S: 1 yard

    For sizes M–XL: 1⅛ yards

- Basic sewing supplies
- Thread to match your fabric
- Ballpoint/jersey needles

SKILLS CHECKLIST

The Basics (Chapter 1, page 9)

Patterns (Chapter 2, page 40)

Basic Techniques (Chapter 2):

- Pinning (page 47)
- Sewing with Knits (page 54)
- Pressing Seams (page 49)
- Sewing in the Round (page 50)
- Setting in Sleeves (page 57)
- Sewing a Neckband (page 55)
- Stretch and Sew (page 54)
- Hemming (page 51)

Your creativity, style, and determination!

CUTTING

Refer to Tracing Patterns (page 41) to trace the DIY Basic Tee Front, Back, and Sleeve patterns (pattern pullout page P1). Cut them out to make your pattern pieces.

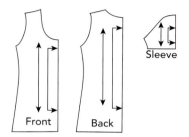

Prewash and iron your fabric before cutting.

Cut out the pieces using the cutting layout at right.

Remember to transfer the pattern markings!

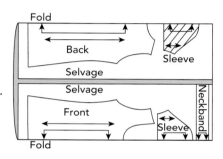

Cut 1 crosswise strip of fabric for the size you are making for the neckband:

XS: 1½˝ × 18¾˝   L: 1½˝ × 21˝

S: 1½˝ × 19½˝   XL: 1½˝ × 21¾˝

M: 1½˝ × 20¼˝

Unfold the fabric layers and separate the pieces from each another. You should end up with 5 pieces total.

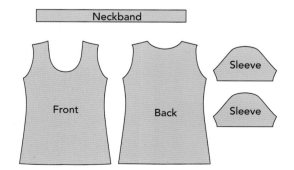

SEWING

Use a ½˝ seam allowance and a zigzag stitch, unless otherwise noted. **This pattern is only suitable for knit fabrics.** *No seam finish is needed for knit fabrics.*

1 Place the back and front right sides together. Match up the shoulder notches and pin the front and back together at both shoulder seams. Sew the shoulder seams. Then pin and sew the 2 side seams.

2 Fold 1 sleeve in half, right sides together, and sew along the straight edge from the top (where it meets the arm-hole) to the bottom. Repeat this step for the other sleeve.

3 Turn both sleeves right side out. Pin a sleeve into 1 of the armholes of the inside-out shirt body. Pin the other sleeve to the remaining armhole. Sew both armhole seams in the round (see Setting in Sleeves, page 57).

4 Sew the neckband to the shirt (see Sewing a Neckband, page 55). Press the neckband flat away from the shirt.

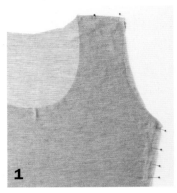

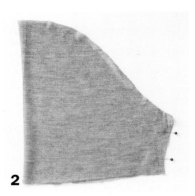

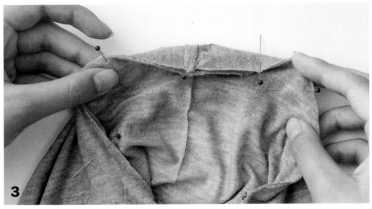

5 Hem the bottom of the tee with a 1˝ hem and the sleeves with a ½˝ hem (see Hemming, page 51). And you're finished! Wasn't that easy?

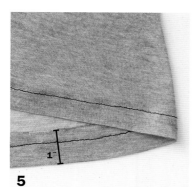

5

PRO TIP

Making this top longer would create a tunic or T-shirt dress, if that's the look you're going for. You could also lengthen or shorten the sleeve to create a cap sleeve, three-quarter-length sleeve, or long sleeve! Just read ahead to Chapter 4 (page 92) to learn how.

CHAPTER 3

SEWING TO FIT YOU

I used to wake up and spend a good twenty minutes finding something to wear. I was frustrated and felt like I had a wardrobe that wasn't wearable. Your closet is most likely full of clothes, yet you still feel you have nothing to wear. Some pieces don't fit your style, while others are falling apart because they were poorly made. Or some just don't suit your lifestyle. By sewing your own clothes, you can avoid all of this.

We want the clothes we create to look as professional as possible, so you'll be learning about seam finishes, which take homemade garments to a whole other level.

You'll also get tips on building your dream wardrobe and making clothes to fit your style.

At the end of this chapter, you'll make a super cute and versatile skater skirt to show off your skills! Ready?

Seam Finishes

If you take a look at a store-bought garment, you'll see that next to the stitching line of the seams is more stitching going around the edge of the fabrics. These **seam finishes** prevent the fabric from fraying.

The cut edges of woven fabrics tend to come undone (fray) over time, which means that finishing your seams is a must, especially once you wash your finished garment. You only need to finish seams with woven fabric because knits don't usually fray. You'll want your beautiful project to last through all the wear and tear. Although not necessary, you'll also want your clothes to feel and look store-bought on the inside as well as the outside. Have I convinced you yet?

Since not all of us have a serger—a sewing machine that can do the special stitch that wraps around the edge found in ready-to-wear (store-bought) clothes—I've come up with a few other options that you can easily do with your regular sewing machine. They work just as well and may look even better. You only need to choose one of the following techniques. In the project instructions, I'll tell you which one I recommend and at which step you should be using it. However, feel free to experiment and play with different options to see which method you like best! At first, this may seem like a waste of time and another step to do, but I promise you, it's totally worth it!

PINKING YOUR SEAMS

This is the fastest and simplest, but not the most effective, seam treatment. Pinking shears are scissors with a zigzag blade. Just trim all the seam allowances with pinking shears. It's best to do this after sewing the garment, so you know you've sewn with the correct seam allowance.

ZIGZAG STITCH SEAM FINISH

The **zigzag stitch seam finish** is the easiest way to finish your seams, and it looks the most similar to ready-to-wear clothing. Use this for both curved and straight seams.

Zigzagged edges

Sew a medium-length zigzag stitch around the edges of the fabric, making sure the edge of the stitch hits right at the edge of the fabric. Go over *all* the raw edges of all the cut pieces and you'll be good to go. It's simple but effective!

The needle hits right at the edge of the fabric

You can also use an overlock stitch (page 30), if your machine has this option.

Overlock stitch

FRENCH SEAMS

French seams look the most professional and are neater than store-bought clothes, but don't let that intimidate you! This method works best for straight or only slightly curved seams and works beautifully on sheer fabrics such as voile or lace. If you choose to use this method, you'll just sew a French seam whenever the instructions say to "sew" certain pieces together.

1 Put your pieces *wrong sides facing* so the right side of the fabric is facing *up*. Sew a ¼˝ seam allowance instead of the usual ½˝. Trim the edges, leaving an ⅛˝ seam.

2 Fold the seam on the stitching line (turn the garment inside out) so the *right* sides are now together.

3 Sew another seam ¼˝ from the folded edge. Iron the seam and voilà! Isn't it beautiful? There aren't any raw edges at all!

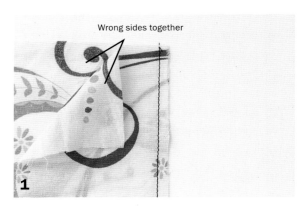

Wrong sides together

1

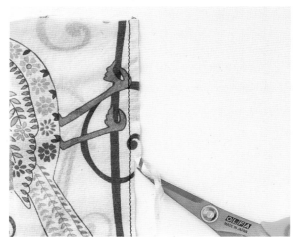

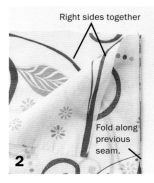

Right sides together

Fold along previous seam.

2

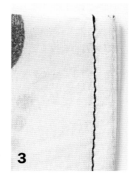

3

Finished French seam, shown from the wrong side

MOCK-FRENCH SEAMS

Mock-French seams look almost exactly like French seams. They're perfect for those instances when you wanted to sew a French seam but forgot to sew the first seam wrong sides together. Best of all, you can also use this seam on curved edges! As with French seams, if you choose to use this method, you'll just sew a mock-French seam whenever the instructions say to "sew" certain pieces together.

1 Sew a regular ½˝ seam as directed. Press the seam open.

2 Fold the raw edges on both sides to meet in the center and press.

3 Put the 2 folds together, pin, and sew ⅛˝ from the original seam to close it up. Very easy but just as clean looking!

Wrong side   Wrong side

1

Fold and press seam allowance to center.

2

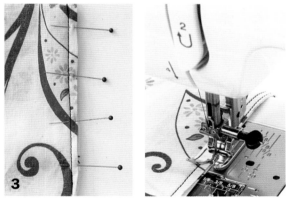

3

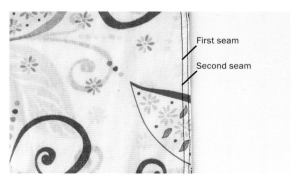

First seam

Second seam

Building Your Dream Wardrobe

When shopping, it's hard to find the perfect pieces we have in mind. By sewing your own clothes, you have the ability to make the exact dress or pants you want. Building your dream wardrobe is not hard; with a few variations to basic patterns, you can easily come up with a closet full of ideas. You may also want to tweak or alter a pattern slightly to your liking. You'll learn how to do this in Chapter 4 (page 75). In the meantime, here are a few style tips and general ideas to keep in mind when planning out a whole new wardrobe of self-made garments.

INSPIRATION

In order to identify your style, gather inspiration. Ideas are everywhere, from the girl you see on the street to a specific city or sight. Don't let these ideas fly away; jot them down. I like to keep a notebook by my side at all times for when inspiration strikes.

Mood boards are also great for a more visual experience. Flip through magazines and cut out images that inspire you. It could be a color, fabric swatch, or style you particularly like. Glue or tape them to a poster board and refer back to them when you need a boost of creativity or something fresh. Take note of what you like and don't like. This will prove useful when developing your style.

STYLE

Style is something I feel very strongly about. Your style represents who you are and who you want to be. It defines your character and personality. Use the inspiration you've gathered to define what you like and how you want to dress. Categorize the pieces you are drawn to into certain styles. Never put yourself in a box, saying that your style is "sophisticated chic" or "floral and feminine." Your style is much more than just a couple of words. Don't be afraid to branch out and try something new. However, you'll often find that there is a particular idea or look you keep coming back to, and that is your style. Most important, stay true to who you are and wear what makes you feel good!

LIFESTYLE

You want the clothes you create to be something you would actually wear. This may mean choosing projects more carefully according to the things you have to do each day. If skirts get in the way when you wear them, go ahead and make a few more pairs of pants. On the other hand, if you love dresses and wear them daily, spend a bit more time making those. The clothes you make should be suited toward your life and lifestyle. The way you dress should be practical and not interfere with your daily activities.

With these simple tips, you'll soon be on the way toward your dream wardrobe!

DIY Skater Skirt

A skirt is a wardrobe staple, and this skirt is no exception. Skater skirts, also called circle skirts, are incredibly popular, and they are super easy to make. There is only one piece to cut out and three seams to sew, which means you'll be making a bunch of these in no time!

The fabric you choose can make a huge impact on the look, so this pattern can turn into anything—from an airy and flowy skirt to a structured and textured skirt. I've made this skirt at a school-appropriate length, so you'll be able to make skirts year-round in all types of fabrics and fibers. Make ten skirts in a row—I won't judge you!

This is also your opportunity to practice the basic skills you've learned since Chapter 1 (page 9) before diving into some serious designing and pro work. Be sure to really learn these techniques, so it'll be a breeze when you start on fancier techniques, including zippers, darts, and designing your own clothes. Let's get started!

FABRIC SUGGESTIONS

The possibilities for this skirt are endless! Use a lightweight or flowy fabric such as lawn or voile for an easy-breezy summer skirt, or go for a thick wool plaid for a super cozy and structured skirt to wear during the colder seasons. You can make this in either a woven or knit fabric and in all weights, heavy or light. All I suggest is to pick something that's not *too* thick so you can avoid a lot of extra bulk. But other than that, go ahead and explore all the possibilities!

SUPPLIES

- Fabric, 60˝ wide:

  Sizes XS–S: 1½ yards

  Sizes M–XL: 1⅔ yards

- 1˝-wide elastic long enough to go around your waist (¾–1 yard depending on your size)
- Basic sewing supplies
- Thread to match your fabric
- Ballpoint/jersey needle if using a knit fabric

SKILLS CHECKLIST

The Basics (Chapter 1, page 9)

Patterns (Chapter 2, page 40)

Basic Techniques (Chapter 2):

- Pinning (page 47)
- Pressing Seams (page 49)
- Sewing in the Round (page 50)
- Stretch and Sew (page 54)
- Hemming (page 51)

Seam Finishes (Chapter 3, page 64)

Your creativity, style, and determination!

CUTTING

Refer to Tracing Patterns (page 41) to trace the DIY Skater Skirt pattern (pullout page P3). Cut it out to make your pattern piece. There is only one piece to this skirt.

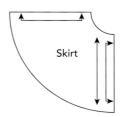

Prewash and iron your fabric. Fold it in half on the lengthwise grain first, and then again on the crosswise grain so you have 4 layers. *For this pattern, you need to make sure both straight edges are on the fabric folds.* Cut out your skirt using the cutting layout below.

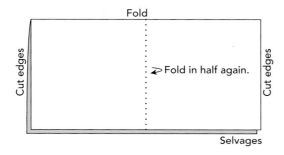

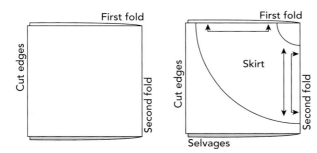

The piece should look like a donut after you unfold it.

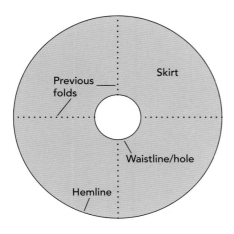

PRO TIP

If you choose to use a slightly see-through fabric, I suggest purchasing another coordinating fabric that's less sheer so you can double the layers. Simply cut two skirts, one out of each fabric, and layer them together to use as one. Sew a basting stitch (page 30) around the edges to keep them together. Continue with the directions and you're good to go!

Seam Finish

If using a woven fabric, use the zigzag stitch seam finish (page 64). Stitch around the inner edges of the donut shape. Finish the bottom if you have a heavier fabric that will only have a single turned hem (Step 8, page 74).

Sewing

Use a ½˝ seam allowance, unless otherwise noted. For knits, use a zigzag stitch.

1 Wrap the elastic around your waist where you plan to wear the skirt. I made mine to sit a little below my natural waist. Find a comfortable fit, making sure the elastic is snug but not too tight. Mark the elastic at the length you like. Add 1˝ to the length and cut the elastic.

Bring the 2 edges of the elastic together and overlap them by 1˝, forming a loop. Make sure the elastic isn't twisted!

Sew a box with an × in the middle on the overlapping elastic ends to connect them. Go over this area a couple of times and remember to backstitch. This section needs to be very secure to last through all the wear and tear.

2 Mark the quarters of the elastic by folding it in half twice and sticking in a pin at each fold. For more detail on how to do this, see Sewing a Neckband, Steps 2 and 3 (page 55).

3 Repeat Step 2 to mark 4 even points on the inner hole of the skirt body.

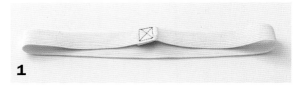

4 Place the elastic inside the skirt so it's facing the wrong side of the fabric. Line the edges of the elastic with the skirt's center hole. Match the pins on the elastic to the markings on the skirt and pin in place.

5 You may notice that the skirt is slightly larger than your elastic. That is perfectly fine, as you are going to stretch the elastic while sewing so it'll fit the skirt. Refer to Stretch and Sew (page 54). Using a zigzag stitch, start at 1 marking and sew the skirt to the elastic close to the raw edge of the fabric, while stretching the elastic to the same length as the skirt between the pins. Sew all the way around, stretching each quarter, until you get back to where you started. Backstitch and cut your threads. The skirt should now be slightly gathered around the elastic.

Skirt wrong side up

6 Fold the elastic down inside the skirt, so you see the right side of the fabric at the waist. Pin in quarters again to hold the elastic down if you need to.

7 Change the machine back to a straight stitch. Working on the inside of the skirt with the wrong side of the fabric facing up, sew the left edge of the elastic down to the skirt body, stretching the elastic as you go. Sew as close to the edge of the elastic as you can. This finishes off the waistband.

8 Depending on your fabric, you can either do a single turned hem (page 51) or a double turned hem (page 51). If you're using a heavy or thick fabric, just fold the bottom edge of the skirt (the outer "ring") up ½″ and topstitch. If you're using a lighter-weight fabric, you can do a narrow double turned hem by folding up the edge ¼″ twice, and then stitch close to the fold. It may take you a while to go all the way around the circumference of the circle, but after that, you're done!

STYLE TIP

You could easily make this skirt high waisted to go with the DIY Boxy Crop Top (page 98). Just measure higher up where you'd like the skirt to sit instead of your normal waist when cutting the elastic—this is usually a smaller measurement. Imagine a matching set with a top and bottom! Super cute and chic! Or try wearing this skirt with an oversized sweater and knee-high boots for fall!

6

7

CHAPTER 4

DESIGN IT

Wow! You've made it through the first three chapters of this book! Now that you've gotten the basic techniques down, give designing your own clothes a try. You'll first sketch out your design. Then I'll guide you through making it come alive. I've covered how to modify patterns to suit your liking, add embellishments such as trims and decorative elastics to your garments, and so much more. I've also included some advanced techniques such as zippers and darts to really help you elevate "homemade" clothes to another level.

Time to make all the items in your dream wardrobe come true! At the end of this chapter, you'll be making a crop top (see DIY Boxy Crop Top, page 98) with the option of turning it into a tank top. Excited yet?

Advanced Techniques

Here are some advanced techniques broken down step-by-step to help you really understand garment construction. These techniques aren't hard; they just look really fancy! They're great for impressing people when you tell them your new dress was made by yourself—just wait 'till they see those gathers and that zipper. ;) It may take you a few tries to get these techniques right, but as always, practice makes perfect!

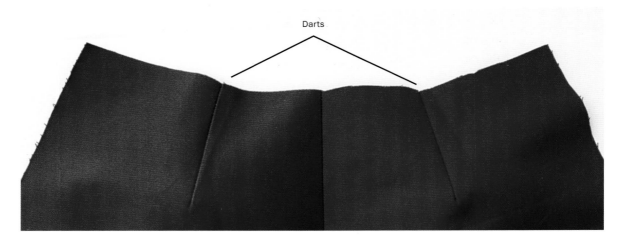

Darts

Ever seen a fitted skirt with two short vertical lines/seams running down from the waist, only to suddenly stop in the middle? Those "lines" are called **darts**. Darts are the funny little triangles of fabric pinched out from the main garment that help create fullness and shape. The human body isn't flat, and we girls especially have more curves, so our clothes have to be tailored to fit them. For example, our bust is often larger than our waist, and in order for fitted tops to be fitted at the waist, darts are used to pinch out the extra fabric at the waist, creating a three-dimensional shape to go out at the bust and in at the waist. Cool, huh?

Darts are usually used on fitted clothing that has little-to-no stretch, but they can also be used on knits to help shape the garment. A fitted blouse, tailored skirt, or body-hugging dress or pants made out of woven fabrics may use darts to fit the garment best to your body. In addition, only women's/junior's clothing have darts, as this group is the one that has curves that really need to be fitted. Younger girls' clothing usually doesn't have darts because that age hasn't begun to develop curves yet.

As described in Pattern Symbols (page 43), the pattern marking for a dart looks like a triangle—sometimes with a line in the middle. Darts are placed symmetrically on most garments, so check to make sure you've marked the darts on both halves or on both pieces of the garment (right and left) before sewing.

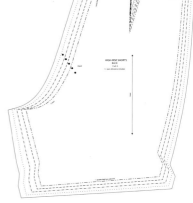

Dart marked accurately

1 Fold the dart in half, right sides of the fabric together, right along the center of the triangle, matching up the slanted lines that form the "legs" of the dart on both sides. Pin through both layers.

2 Beginning at the wide end of the dart, sew using a straight stitch, following the slanted line all the way until the tip and going off the edge of the fabric without backstitching. Cut the threads, leaving long tails.

3 Tie the tails of the threads into a double knot. Backstitching causes unwanted bumps, so by double knotting the threads, you get a clean finish and point. Trim the threads.

4 Lay the dart flat and press the folded edge flat on an ironing board.

5 Open up the fabric and press the dart flat in the direction stated in the instructions (or see Pressing, page 49, for general guidelines).

6 Use a tailor's ham or a rolled-up towel and press the tip of the dart from the right side of the fabric as shown to help shape the piece to match the curve of the body. You may want to use steam here.

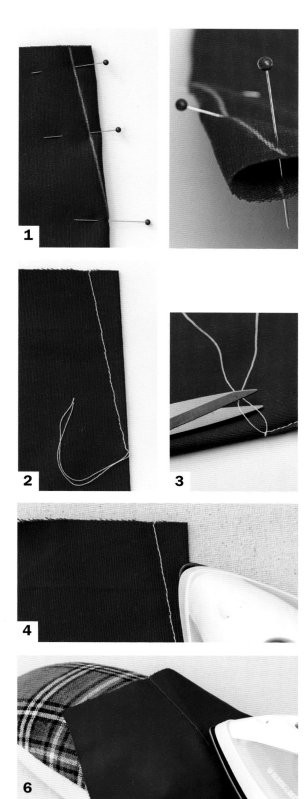

GATHERS

I'm sure you've seen **gathers** before and know how pretty they can be. Gathers can be found everywhere, such as gathered skirts, gathered tops, baby-doll dresses, and so on. A narrow strip of fabric that is gathered is called a ruffle. Ready?

1 Pull the bobbin and top threads on your sewing machine so you have a long tail of thread to start with. Using the longest stitch on your machine (a basting stitch, page 30), sew 2 or 3 lines of stitching onto the fabric right side up. Leave a long tail of thread at the other end. Do not backstitch. The first line should be ⅛˝ from the edge, the second line ⅛˝ away from the first line, and the third line ⅛˝ away from the second line. *Note: Contrasting thread used here for visibility. The black thread is the upper thread, and the red thread is the bobbin thread.*

1

2 On the wrong side of the fabric, pull the bobbin threads of the basting. Pull equally on all 3 threads to gather the fabric, sliding the fabric along the threads until the ruffled piece is the same length as the piece it is going to be sewn to.

3 Pin the ends and then the entire length of the gathered pieces to the main fabric, right sides together. Stitch the seam indicated in the instructions, with the gathered side up, so you know what you're doing. Carefully use your fingers to help the gathers lie flat as they go through the machine. Once the seam is sewn, remove any basting stitches that show on the right side. Give the seam a good press and that's all there is to it!

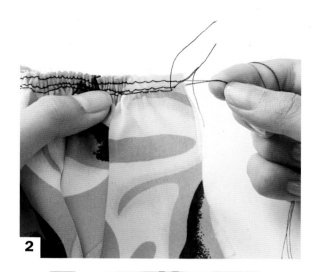

2

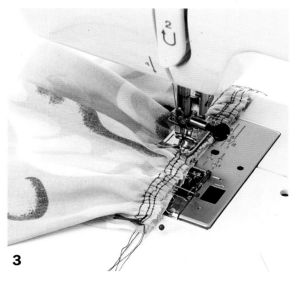

3

BIAS BINDING

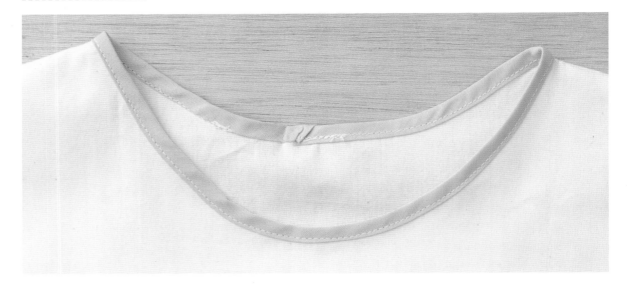

Bias bindings are used to finish visible edges, such as necklines and armholes, so they don't fray. You create a bias binding by using strips of fabric called **bias tape**. Bias tape is really just regular fabric cut on the bias to create stretch to go around curved edges; it is then folded in a way to be easily sewn. You can make bias tape or buy it from the fabric store in cute little packages of solid trim. The supply list for a project should say how wide the bias tape should be and how much of it you will need. If you're buying it, be sure to look for the kind that says "double-fold bias tape," which is the kind we'll be using in this book. If you want to make your own (which is so much cuter), I'll teach you how in Making Bias Tape (page 82). *It's a good idea to practice attaching the bias tape on a scrap of fabric with a straight edge before you move on to garments.*

Store-bought bias tape—kind of boring, if you ask me

ATTACHING BIAS BINDING

1 Unfold the bias tape with the wrong side of fabric facing up.

2 On the right side of the garment, sandwich the raw edge you are binding (neckline or armhole) between the layers of the bias tape as shown. Pin all the way around, leaving a 2″–3″ tail on both ends unpinned. Check to make sure the folded edges are even, because you'll be sewing on both sides in 1 step.

3 Stitch close to the edge of the bias tape. Make sure when you're sewing that you're catching the other folded edge on the wrong side of the garment. Stop about 1″ or so from where the 2 ends of the tape would meet. Some machines have special binding feet to make this easier.

Wrong side up

1

2

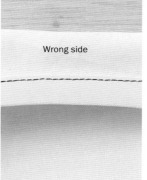

3

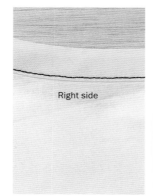
Right side

Wrong side

4 To join the 2 ends together, cut off any excess bias tape, leaving about an inch extra. Fold the loose end of the tape under ½˝ to the wrong side. Overlap the edges and finish sewing down the last bit of the bias tape. Press the fold so it lies flat.

MAKING BIAS TAPE

Bias tape can give you a really clean and professional finish with just a couple of seams. When the tape is made with the same fabric as the garment, you can get a really polished and simple look. You can also use a contrasting fabric for decorative purposes. Store-bought bias tape is handy when you're in a rush, but it usually only comes in select solid colors and limited fabrics. It's very easy to make your own, and then the options become endless! You'll have so many more choices in prettier colors and prints!

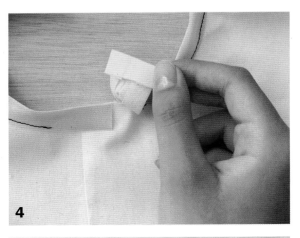

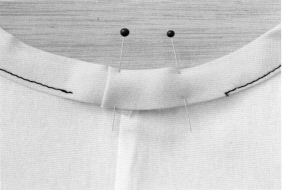

4

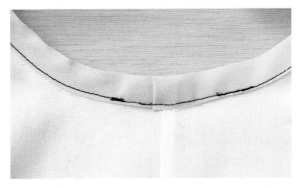

1 Cut a square out of woven fabric. I suggest you use 100% cotton, cotton-poly blends, or polyester prints. See the chart (page 84) to tell you what size square to cut for the amount of bias tape you want to make. Smaller patterns work the best (as you can see, the bird on my fabric had its body chopped in half, haha). Draw a line from corner to corner and cut along that line.

2 To figure out how wide you should cut your bias tape, take the measurement you want the finished bias tape to be and multiply it by 4. For example, to make $\frac{1}{2}$″-wide bias tape: $\frac{1}{2}$″ × 4 = 2″. This is a common size for garment sewing.

3 On both triangles, draw lines parallel to the diagonal cut edge spaced the amount apart that you figured out in Step 2.

4 Cut along the lines to create strips on the bias.

5 To join the strips, place the short ends right sides together shown. Pin and sew a diagonal line across. Cut off the excess fabric, leaving about a $\frac{1}{4}$″ seam allowance. Press the seam open. Keep on going until you have a long strip.

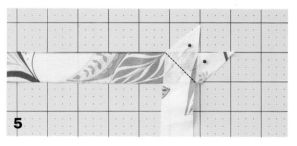

6 Fold the long edges of the bias strip to the wrong side, meeting at the center. As you fold, press the folds so they stay in place. A bias tape maker is an inexpensive tool that makes this much faster and easier—you just slide the tape into it, and it creates the folds that you then iron in place. Turn off the steam on your iron so you don't burn your fingers!

7 Fold the strip in half again so no raw edges are showing. Press, and that's all there's to it! I like to wrap my finished tape around pieces of cardboard for easy storage and less tangling.

LENGTH OF ¼"-WIDE BIAS TAPE	YARDAGE NEEDED	CUT SIZE OF FABRIC SQUARE
1 yard	⅓ yard	10½˝ × 10½˝
1½ yards	⅜ yard	12½˝ × 12½˝
2 yards	⅜ yard	13½˝ × 13½˝
2½ yards	½ yard	14½˝ × 14½˝
3 yards	½ yard	15½˝ × 15½˝
3½ yards	½ yard	16½˝ × 16½˝
4 yards	½ yard	16½˝ × 16½˝
LENGTH OF ½"-WIDE BIAS TAPE		
1 yard	⅜ yard	13½˝ × 13½˝
1½ yards	½ yard	15½˝ × 15½˝
2 yards	½ yard	16½˝ × 16½˝
2½ yards	⅝ yard	18½˝ × 18½˝
3 yards	⅝ yard	19½˝ × 19½˝
3½ yards	⅝ yard	20½˝ × 20½˝
4 yards	⅝ yard	21½˝ × 21½˝

INSERTING A ZIPPER

Zippers can really make a dress or pair of pants look professional and store-bought. Unlike other methods, a centered zipper is the easiest to install, with no weird puckering or gaps. This is how zippers are installed in the projects in this book, such as the DIY High-Rise Shorts (page 112). All you'll need is the zipper with the indicated length and some patience. There are different types of zippers, so check the package to make sure you are buying the right type for your project. For most dresses, pants, and skirts, you will want a nylon coil zipper with a locking pull and a closed bottom.

If you can't find a zipper the length you need, you can buy a nylon zipper in a longer length and shorten it by measuring the desired length and sewing a bar tack (at right) across the teeth to create a new zipper stop. Then cut off the rest of the zipper below the bar tack.

A **bar tack** is a wide stitch sewn back and forth several times. You can sew it by hand or by machine using a wide zigzag stitch with a length of 0 (look in your sewing machine manual for the correct settings.)

1 Make sure the seam you're inserting the zipper into is already sewn or basted closed.

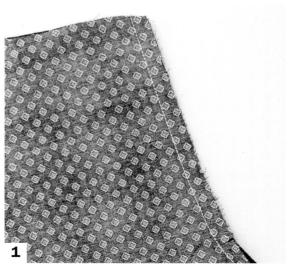

1

2 Press the seam open and place the zipper face down, centered on the seam, with the teeth lining up with the seam and the top of the pull aligned with what will be the top finished edge of your garment (so leave the amount of the seam allowance free). Pin the tape on both sides of the teeth.

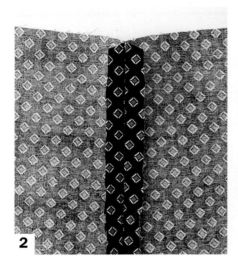

3 Put the zipper foot on your sewing machine. Working on the wrong side of the garment and starting from the upper right-hand edge of the zipper, sew along the side all the way until the zipper stop. Lift the presser foot, rotate the garment, and then lower the foot and sew across the bottom of the zipper where the zipper stop is. Then lift the presser foot, rotate, lower it again, and sew back up the other side of the zipper. If the zipper pull is in your way, just stop stitching for a moment and slide it up or down the zipper to make sewing a lot easier.

The arrows show the direction you will be stitching.

4 On the right side, snip or use a seam ripper to remove the threads holding the seam together on top of the zipper, revealing the zipper underneath. Stop just above the zipper stop. Using small, sharp scissors may be easier than using a seam ripper.

5 Sew a bar tack right underneath the zipper stop by using a wide zigzag stitch with a length of 0.0 (stitching in place) to prevent the rest of the seam from coming undone. Press with low heat; melted zippers smell horrible, trust me!

4

5

The Design Concept

If you take a look in your closet, you'll see that many of your clothes are variations of one another. Maybe your favorite items are your super soft tees, and though they're all really soft and are tees, one shirt may have a round neckline and another has a V-neck. One of them is black, while the others are in pastel colors. The black tee is more of a T-shirt dress than T-shirt, while the pastel ones are a little cropped. These little things are all **design elements** that someone (the designer) must have chosen.

Fabric choices, neckline (round, V-neck, scoop), sleeve length (short, three-quarter, long), overall length (tunic, regular, cropped), overall fit (tight, loose, semi-fitted), and the shape of the garment (A-line, boxy, slim). They're all variations. It's the same idea when you're making the garment itself. You start with a basic pattern, like the ones I've included in this book, and you'll make changes to the pattern to adjust them to your design. The basic pattern acts as your base; then you'll add details and small changes to make the garment really "you." Almost all of your design will start with this base.

Sketching

Drawing out your design before making your garment is very important in the design process. It lets you see what you're going for before jumping right in. If you're anything like me, you think you can't draw, so you may be freaking out now. Stay calm. Your drawing doesn't have to be super detailed or a work of art; it just needs to be clear enough that you know what you're doing. Nobody ever has to see your sketch, so it can be as rough as it can get. Just do it!

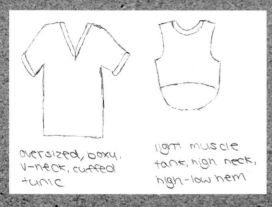

oversized, boxy, V-neck, cuffed tunic

light muscle tank, high neck, high-low hem

Choose the design elements for your design and draw them out in your sketch.

Do you want this dress to have a knee-length skirt or something a little shorter? A V-neck or crewneck? Long sleeves or short sleeves? How about the fit: oversized or tight? Include all of these details while drawing. You can also write down any notes and supplies you'll need. That way, you can just take this sketch to the fabric store to help you find the right materials.

Sketch to Final Product

The process of going from sketch to finished garment goes something a little like this:

1 **Sketching:** Design the garment.

2 **Analyzing the pattern, fit, and design:** Find a base pattern similar to the final design, figure out the differences between the pattern and design, such as fit, length, sleeve design, and shape.

3 **Modifying the pattern:** Make the necessary changes to the base pattern to turn it into a pattern that can be used for the designed garment. Changes could include lengthening/shortening the length, adding/removing width (to make it looser or more fitted), and adding decorative elements, such as necklines or collars.

4 **Making the garment:** Once the changes are made to the pattern, that pattern can now be used to make the garment.

We've already talked about sketching and the techniques used to make clothes, but analyzing and modifying patterns is really where the magic happens. It's where a very basic design can be made into something very artistic and show-stopping. People often overlook these steps, but without a specialized pattern, a complex design and sewing techniques can't serve their purpose.

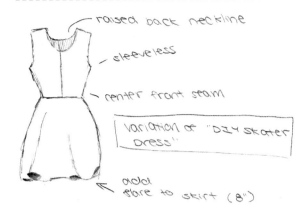

raised back neckline

sleeveless

center front seam

variation of "DIY skater dress"

add flare to skirt (8")

When choosing a pattern to act as the "base," be realistic. Don't expect to transform a super baggy top into something tight and fitted. Adjustments can be made, but adding or decreasing the width too much can distort the pattern. Pick a pattern that's similar in fit, and figure out what needs to be changed.

Make a list, describing the elements that need to be altered and how much you would like to add/subtract to it. The sleeves need to be a little longer? How much longer? The skirt should be a little more flared? By a few inches? Or around 10˝? Note all these details and write down the measurements for how much each section needs to be altered.

The patterns in this book are pretty forgiving in terms of fit, but as I said before, I don't recommend drastically changing the pattern. I would say 12˝ widthwise and lengthwise is the maximum.

It helps if you've already made the base pattern into a garment, because then you can try it on and see how much you would like to increase or decrease in inches. For example, let's say you want a low V-neck on a top, but the base pattern has a high round neck. If you can try on the garment made from the base pattern, you can measure how many inches the neck needs to be lowered.

Before making any changes to the base pattern, I recommend tracing a copy of the pattern instead of making the changes directly onto it. You've already traced a copy of it in your size (the pattern you're currently using), but having another copy is great when you want to make multiple variations off of one base pattern. One pattern, many designs.

After altering your pattern, remember to label what pattern it is and what modifications you made to it so you can reuse it in the future. Also note that after modifying the pattern, you may need more or less fabric to make the garment because of the added or decreased length/width. My best tip would be to lay out all your modified pattern pieces to estimate how much fabric you're going to need.

I suggest that for the more modified patterns, you make a muslin (a test garment cut from inexpensive fabric) to test the fit and make any extra pattern adjustments before moving onto your good fabric. You don't have to do any hems, seam finishes, or closures on the muslin. You just want to see how your changes work out on your body before you commit to that special fabric that you only have so much of.

ADJUSTING THE NECKLINE

This is probably the easiest adjustment to make. It's pretty self-explanatory: use this technique when you want to change the neckline of any top or dress.

1 Starting with the front piece of the base pattern, where the center front meets the neckline, measure and make a mark where the finished neckline needs to be. For the following examples, I'm raising and lowering the neckline by 1˝. If you're raising the neckline, you can tape/glue another piece of paper where the neckline is to make the marking. Be sure to also make a mark where the shoulder and neckline meet, ½˝ down from the shoulder seam.

Marking 1˝ higher neckline

Marking 1˝ lower neckline

2 Draw a curve for a round neck or a straight line for a V-neck, connecting the shoulder mark to the center front mark. This creates a new neckline.

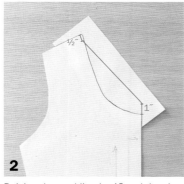

Raising the neckline by 1˝ and drawing a straight line, creating a V-neck

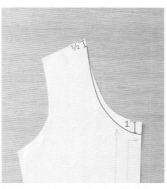

Lowering the neckline by 1˝ and drawing a curved line, creating a round neck

PRO TIP

When changing the neckline, you also need to change the length of the neckband (the band that goes around your neck on T-shirts), since drawing a new neckline either increases or decreases the circumference of the neck hole. A good rule of thumb is to measure the circumference of the new neckline and cut the neckband 2˝–2½˝ shorter than that measurement.

LENGTHENING AND SHORTENING

It's really easy to add length or to shorten the length. This technique can be used on tops, dresses, sleeves, pants, shorts, and skirts—almost everything you can imagine. For two-piece garments such as dresses (made out of a bodice and a skirt), you can choose the length of the bodice or the skirt—or both. Lengthening the bodice will create a low waist, while lengthening the skirt will make a longer skirt. It's all up to the design!

1 Find the pattern piece that corresponds to what needs to be altered. For example, I'm trying to lengthen/shorten the sleeves of a dress, so I'm working on the sleeve pattern piece. Then look for the "lengthen or shorten here" line on the pattern.

2 Cut along that line, creating 2 pieces.

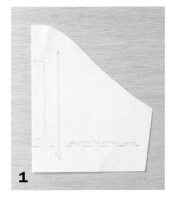

3 To lengthen, tape a piece of paper in between the cut pieces that is equal to how much the piece needs to be lengthened. For example, I taped a 2˝-wide strip of paper to lengthen the sleeve by 2˝.

To shorten the piece, overlap the 2 pattern pieces by half of what needs to be subtracted. For example, I'm shortening the sleeve by 2˝, so 2˝ × ½ = 1˝. I overlapped the pieces by 1˝ and taped them together. If you are using commercial patterns on tissue paper, you can also fold the patterns to shorten them.

If there are any jagged edges, just smooth them out by drawing a straight line to connect the top to the bottom. That's all!

Lengthening sleeve by 2˝

Shortening sleeve by 2˝

ADDING AND SUBTRACTING MINIMAL WIDTH

This technique is for when you want to adjust the width (really, the circumference, or the distance all the way around) on a garment by a little (as in 2˝ or less). You can use this technique at the bust, the waist, the sleeve, or even a pant leg. This method is easier and less fuss than other ways of adjusting the width, such as slashing and spreading (page 95), which is used for adjusting by more than 2˝.

1 Figure out how much width you want to add or remove.

2 Count how many seams are in the part of the garment you are adjusting. For a top, skirt, or the waist of pants or shorts, that is usually 2 seams. For a sleeve or pants, that is usually 1 seam.

3 Multiply the number of seams by 2 (because there are 2 pieces of fabric in each seam).

4 Divide the amount from Step 1 by the number from Step 3 to determine the amount to adjust the pattern at each seam. I'll call this number x.

5 Starting with the front piece of the pattern and following the side seam, mark x in to decrease the width or x out to increase the width. Tape on another piece of paper if necessary. Use your ruler to measure and make markings along the line that creates the side seam.

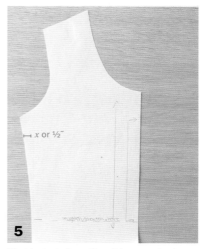

Marking x in from the side seam to decrease the width

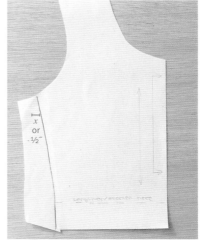

Marking x out from the side seam to increase the width

6 Connect all the markings to create a new side line.

7 Repeat Steps 2 and 3 on the back piece, decreasing/increasing the same width on the side seam.

8 If the seam you change will be sewn to another part of the garment (like a dress bodice to a skirt or a shirt to a sleeve), you will need to make a similar decrease/increase to the connecting pattern pieces. So if you removed ½˝ from the side of a dress bodice, mark the same change on the skirt piece where it meets the bodice. If the dress has sleeves, also remove ½˝ from the sleeve side seam. Then draw a new line connecting the new point to the opposite end of the existing seam. *Remember, you only want to make this change where the seam meets the changed pattern piece, so mark only 1 point to change, not 2. Otherwise you will change more than you intended.*

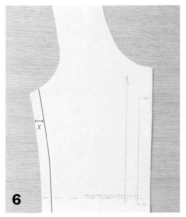
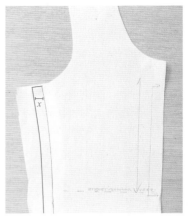

Width decreased   Width increased

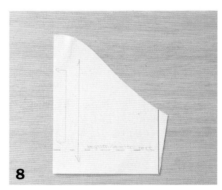

Removing ½˝ from sleeve where it meets the dress to fit a dress taken in 2˝

PRO TIP

The reason I had you divide the original amount for tops and bottoms by 4 in Step 1 (page 93) is because that width will be quadrupled when cut from fabric. See, we're only working on a quarter of the garment: the front pattern piece is only half of the front of our bodies, which is half of the circumference of our bodies. The x gets doubled when added to the side seam on the other side of our body and doubled again when added to both sides of our back. It's sort of like a shirt being folded in half and then in half again. The shirt is now only a quarter of what it used to be.

Think of how many seams you will be changing. For shorts/pant legs, there's only one front and one back piece per leg, so the amount is divided by 2, not 4. With a sleeve pattern like the ones in the book, you also divide by 2 because you are adding to each side of the one side seam.

Adjusting Width by "Slashing and Spreading"

Slashing and spreading sounds a little scary and awkward, but I promise you it's not. This method for adjusting width takes longer and is more tedious than the technique in Adding and Subtracting Minimal Width (page 93). However, it will give you more accuracy for adjustments 3˝ or greater because the width is divided evenly throughout the pattern, rather than all added from the side. Note that this method is mostly used for *adding* a flared shape or *increasing* the width for a *section* of the garment, such as adding width to the bottom of the skirt to create more of a flare. If you want the entire garment to be looser or tighter, I suggest making the garment in a size larger or smaller.

1 For tops or skirts: Determine how much needs to be added to the width and divide that by 4 because of what you just learned in the Pro Tip (page 94). For example, I'm adding 12˝ to the bottom and top, so 12˝ ÷ 4 = 3˝. I'm left with 3˝.

Divide that number by 3. For example, 3˝ ÷ 3 = 1˝, so my finished measurement is 1˝. From now on, this number will be called x.

So, the formula (the mathematical way to figure this out) for tops/skirts is:

x = (width that needs to be added / subtracted ÷ 4) ÷ 3

For pants or shorts: Follow the instructions above, but divide by 2 instead of 4.

x = (width that needs to be added / subtracted ÷ 2) ÷ 3.

2 Working with the front piece of the pattern, divide the upper edge (in my case, near the neckline / arm hole / shoulder seam) into 4 equal sections and mark them. Divide the bottom edge (where the width is going to be altered) into 4 equal sections.

3 Draw lines to connect the markings on the top edge to those on the bottom edge. You should end up with 3 lines running vertically up and down on the pattern. Extend the lines so they reach the very top and bottom of the pattern if needed.

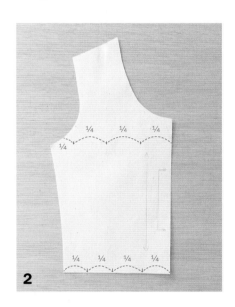

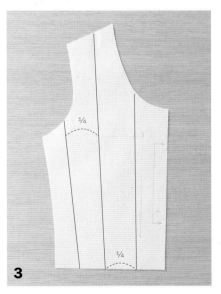

4 Cut on the lines, starting from the bottom and going up. Leave ⅛″ uncut at the top edge, creating a paper "hinge." This is where the "slash" in "slashing and spreading" happens.

5 Lay the slashed pattern over a large piece of paper. Spread (aha! the "spreading" part appears) the bottom edge of the cut panels, leaving your measurement x in between the panels. Tape down the pieces to secure them in place.

Now you just need to smooth out any weird angles or curves by connecting or redrawing them. Once you're done, you can cut out the pattern from the sheet of paper.

6 Repeat Steps 2–5 on the back piece of the pattern.

Pro Tip

This method can also be used to add width to the overall fit. Although making the garment in a size larger is certainly easy, it doesn't always fit your needs. (For example, no matter how large of a size you make a pair of super skinny pants, they still won't be loose enough to be a pair of sweatpants.) To adjust the overall fit, cut on the lines entirely in Step 5; don't leave ⅛″ uncut. Cut through the entire line. Spread the pattern, leaving the same amount between the panels at the upper edge as at the lower edge.

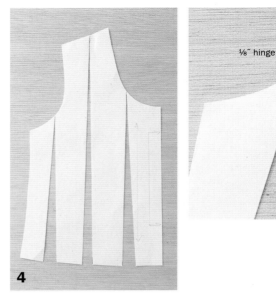

⅛″ hinge

4

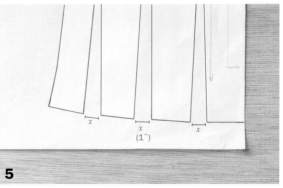

x x x
(1″)

5

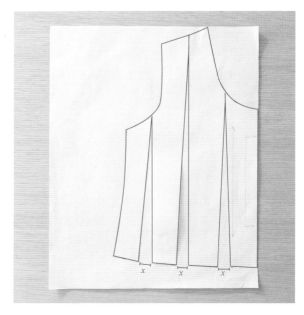

x x x

EMBELLISHMENTS

Embellishments are a fun way to add personality to your design. Clothes that you make yourself are definitely special, but adding cool trims, buttons, and beads can really turn your garments into works of art. Or add them for fun! A simple search on Pinterest (pinterest.com) could lead to thousands of great ideas. The following examples are just a couple to get you started.

NOTE

When you create your Pinterest account, you must provide them with accurate and complete information. Any use or access by anyone under the age of thirteen is prohibited.

FABRIC PAINT

Fabric paint is great for painting cool designs on fabric, since not all fabrics come in the exact printed design you want. Some of my suggestions are to paint an **ombre** (a fancy word for solid colors gradually transitioning into another—usually a lighter shade turning into a darker shade) on a solid-colored garment or to use a stencil to create a graphic print. It's a good idea to test your paint on a scrap of the fabric first to make sure it won't make the fabric stiff or crackly. Always follow the manufacturer's instructions to care for the finished painted fabric, so it will last.

TRIMS AND BUTTONS

Fabric stores have all kinds of trims, from pom-poms to fringe to rickrack. There's also an endless section of ribbons, including metallics and satins. These trims and ribbons can simply be topstitched on after the garment is finished. Buttons can also be used decoratively, for a little something-something!

PRO TIP

Use Fray Check (a type of clear glue) to keep the ends of trim and ribbons from fraying before you stitch them on.

OTHER

Studs, beads, and decorative stitching (by hand or with your sewing machine) are some other ways you can decorate your garments. Strips of fabric can be gathered to create ruffles, while zippers can be topstitched onto a shirt just as a fun, finishing touch. The possibilities are really endless, so have fun with it!

DIY Boxy Crop Top

This little crop top will be your go-to staple during warmer weather, and it's perfect with the DIY High-Rise Shorts (page 112) or the DIY Skater Skirt (page 69). It can also be worn in colder climates when made in a cozy fabric and paired with high-waisted jeans and an oversized coat. This top is quite easy to make—easier than you think and really similar to the DIY Basic Tee (page 60).

FABRIC SUGGESTIONS

Any kind of woven—or even nonwoven—fabric will work for this top. As long as there's no stretch, whatever you choose will turn out beautiful. My top was made from a sparkly sequined mesh fabric to create something more formal, but by using a lightweight cotton voile, lawn, or linen, you could make something more suitable for everyday wear. Other nontraditional options include flannel, lightweight wool, faux leather, lace, and chiffon.

SUPPLIES

- Woven or non-stretchy fabric:

  XS-S, 45˝ wide: 1½ yards   XS-S, 60˝ wide: 1 yard

  M-XL, 45˝ wide: 1¾ yards   M-XL, 60˝ wide: 1⅛ yards

- 1 yard of woven or non-stretchy fabric

- 7½ yards bias tape or seam binding if using sequined fabric *(optional)*

- Basic sewing supplies, including a hand sewing needle

- Thread to match your fabric

SKILLS CHECKLIST

The Basics (Chapter 1, page 9)

Patterns (Chapter 2, page 40)

Basic Techniques (Chapter 2):

- Pinning (page 47)
- Pressing Seams (page 49)
- Sewing in the Round (page 50)
- Setting in Sleeves (page 57)
- Sewing a Neckband (page 55)
- Hemming (page 51)
- Bias Binding (page 80)

Depending on the fabric chosen:

   Seam Finishes (Chapter 3, page 64)

   OR

   Advanced Techniques (Chapter 4, page 75)

Your creativity, style, and determination!

CUTTING

Refer to Tracing Patterns (page 41) to trace the DIY Boxy Crop Top Front, Back, and Sleeve patterns (pattern pullout page P2). Cut them out to make your pattern pieces.

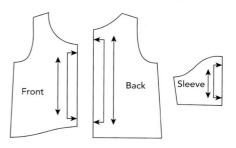

Prewash and press your fabric, unless you're using a dry-clean-only fabric like the sequin fabric I used. Cut out the pieces for your top using the following cutting layout. Remember to transfer the pattern markings!

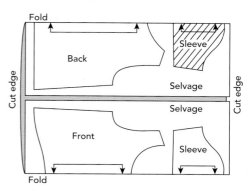

Layout shown for 60˝ wide fabric

Continued on page 100

Continued from page 99

Also cut a strip of fabric for the size you are
making for the neckband:

- XS: 1½″ × 26¾″

- S: 1½″ × 27⅛″

- M: 1½″ × 28″

- L: 1½″ × 28⅝″

- XL: 1½″ × 29⅜″

Unfold the fabric layers and separate the pieces
from each other. You should end up with 5 pieces
total.

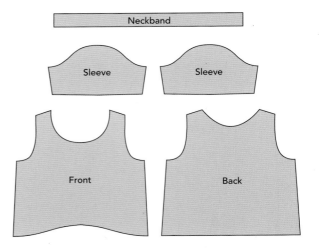

SEAM FINISHING

You can finish all the seam allowances in advance
or wait until after you sew each seam. You can use
the zigzag stitch seam finish (page 65) over the
raw edges of the pieces before continuing, sew
mock-French seams (page 67) as you go along, or
use bias binding (page 80) on all of your seams,
which is what I did to prevent the sequins on my
top from falling all over the place.

SEWING

*Use a ½″ seam allowance, unless
otherwise noted.*

1 Place the front and back pieces
right sides together and sew the
shoulders and sides together.

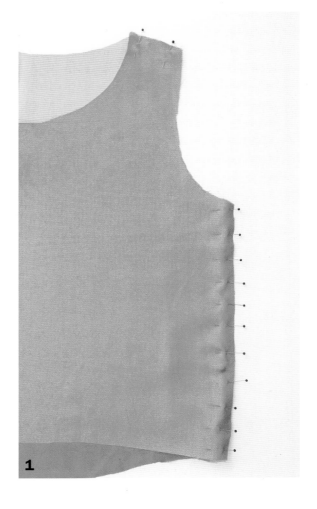

1

2 Fold the sleeves in half and sew the side seam.

3 Pin the sleeves into the armholes, with right sides together, and sew the armhole seam.

4 Fold the neckband in half, right sides together, matching the long raw edges to create a skinny strip. Press.

5 Hand sew large basting stitches (page 30) in the fold. Pull the thread to gather the fold *ever so slightly*. Just a little. With knit fabrics, you can stretch a smaller neckband to fit the neckline, but since wovens don't stretch, this is the easiest way to prevent gaping at the upper edge.

2

3

4

5

6 Sew the short ends of the neckband together, creating a ring. Fold it back in half, right sides together. With the body right side out, pin the raw edges of the band to the shirt's neckline. Sew in the round (page 50) along the entire neckline.

6

7 Press the neckband away from the shirt body.

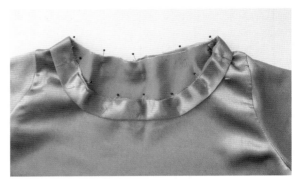

8 Hem the sleeves by doing a ¼˝ double turned hem (page 51). Note that I had to do a single turned hem (page 51) because the sequins prevented me from turning the edge twice. Hem the bottom edge of the shirt by turning under ¼˝ and then 1˝. Voilà, you just made a top!

7

MAKE IT YOUR OWN

FLARED TANK TOP

An easy-breezy tank top is a must-have basic in every girl's wardrobe. It's best made in lighter-weight fabrics. Turning the DIY Boxy Crop Top (page 98) into a tank only requires a couple of simple modifications. I made the top longer by lengthening (page 92) the front and back pattern pieces by about 5˝. I also evened out the curve of the front hemline and drew a curve on the back hemline to create a high-low effect, added width to the hemline of the top by slashing and spreading (page 95), and lowered the armhole line a little for ease.

STYLE TIP

To make this top more interesting, add some fun trim such as lace or fringe! Or you could cut this tank on the bias (placing the grainline on a 45° angle) to make a really pretty, flowy top that will complement your curves. The pieces may be trickier to sew with the natural stretch of fabric when cut on the bias, but it'll be worth it!

CHAPTER 5

MORE PROJECTS AND INSPIRATION

This chapter includes some other fun projects to keep you busy and help you build more of your dream wardrobe, such as a dress and shorts. In addition to the projects, I came up with some possible variations and included how I modified the patterns. These are just ideas; you are free to experiment and modify the design however you like. Try taking a sketch and turning it into a real-life garment by following the design process. You'll soon be on your way to a full collection of clothes you designed, made yourself, and love! Have fun!

DIY Skater Dress

There's nothing more satisfying than wearing an entire outfit made by you. A dress is exactly that, since all you need is a dress and, well, you're dressed! This skater dress is really comfy to wear yet still really cute. Simple and stylish, the fit-and-flare silhouette will look great on any body shape. Make a couple in cotton jersey for everyday wear or one in a stretch velvet for special occasions. Ready to make your first dress?

FABRIC SUGGESTIONS

Use a knit fabric with nice stretch and recovery (the ability to spring back into shape after stretching). Jersey, interlock, stretch lace, and double knits will all work as long as they're stretchy enough. If you can find a super stretchy velvet or stretch faux leather, either one will make a beautiful, show-stopping dress. Be careful not to pick something that's too thin or lightweight, since the dress is form-fitting—you don't want any undergarment lines peeking through! In addition, knits without much stretch mean the waist may not fit over your shoulders, so if you do choose a more stable knit, make the dress in a size larger.

SUPPLIES

- Knit fabric, 60˝ wide:

  Sizes XS–M: ½ yard for top and ½–1 yard for skirt

  Sizes L–XL: ⅝ yard for top and ½–1 yard for skirt

  Skirt yardage will vary depending on your individual skirt pattern.

- Basic sewing supplies

- Ballpoint/jersey needles

- Thread to match your fabric

SKILLS CHECKLIST

The Basics (Chapter 1, page 9)

Patterns (Chapter 2, page 40)

Basic Techniques (Chapter 2):

- Pinning (page 47)
- Sewing with Knits (page 54)
- Pressing Seams (page 49)
- Sewing in the Round (page 50)
- Setting in Sleeves (page 57)
- Sewing a Neckband (page 55)
- Stretch and Sew (page 54)
- Hemming (page 51)

Sketch to Final Product (Chapter 4):

- Analyzing Pattern, Fit, and Design (page 90)
- Basics of Modifying Patterns (page 91)
- Slashing and Spreading (page 95)

Your creativity, style, and determination!

CUTTING

Refer to Tracing Patterns (page 41) to trace the DIY Skater Dress Front/Back and Sleeve patterns (pattern pullout page P3). Cut them out to make your patterns.

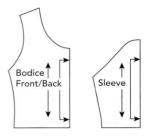

For the skirt portion of the dress, you'll draft your own pattern following the illustrations.

Draw a rectangle where the width equals your waist divided by 2 and the length equals the length of the skirt.

Divide the width of the rectangle evenly into 3 sections. Draw a grainline through the center of the middle section, parallel to the width of the rectangle. Cut apart the rectangle on the 2 inner lines, leaving ⅛″ uncut at one side. This will act like a hinge to keep the top of the skirt pattern together.

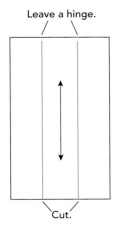

Leave a hinge.

Cut.

Put the cut-open rectangle on a larger piece of paper.

Spread out the cut panels and leave 6″–10″ of space between the bottom of the panels. Trace the outside shape, smoothing out the lines.

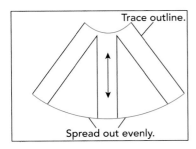

Trace outline.

Spread out evenly.

Cut out the piece and label it as your skirt pattern.

Prewash and iron your fabric. Lay out the pattern pieces as shown in the cutting layout.

Also cut a strip of fabric for the size you are making for the neckband:

- XS: 1½″ × 21¼″
- S: 1½″ × 22″
- M: 1½″ × 22¾″
- L: 1½″ × 23½″
- XL: 1½″ × 24¼″

The patterns shown with an asterisk and diagonal lines mean you should cut the pattern piece right side up first (making sure not to cut on the "fold" line) and then unpin it, flip it over, and finish cutting the rest of the shape. You can also cut out the skirt piece first and then fold the fabric together on the selvages to cut the remaining pieces on the fold if you have enough fabric.

Skirt

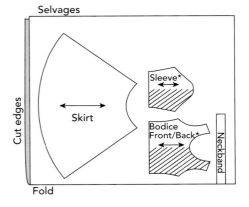

Selvages

Cut edges

Skirt

Sleeve*

Bodice Front/Back*

Neckband

Fold

Unfold the fabric layers and separate the pieces from each other. You should end up with 7 pieces total.

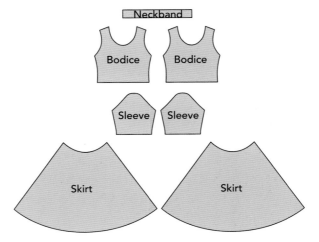

Neckband

Bodice

Bodice

Sleeve

Sleeve

Skirt

Skirt

SEWING

Use a ½˝ seam allowance and a zigzag stitch, unless otherwise noted. **This pattern is only suitable for knit fabrics.** *No seam finish is needed for knit fabrics.*

1 Place the front and back pieces right sides together. Pin and sew the shoulder seams. Then place the front and back side seams together and pin and sew the seam.

2 Fold the sleeves in half as shown; pin and sew the side seams.

3 Pin the sleeves into the armholes, right sides together, matching the notches, and sew the armhole seam, referring to Setting in Sleeves (page 57) as needed.

Fold.

1

2

3

4 Refer to Sewing a Neckband (page 55) to make the neckband. Sew it to the bodice neckline using a ¼˝ seam allowance instead of ½˝. Press the neckband away from the bodice and the seam allowances toward the bodice. Set the bodice aside for now.

5 Match up the skirt pieces, right sides together. Pin and sew both side seams.

6 Switch the machine back to a straight stitch and hem the sleeves by folding 1˝ of the raw edge under to the inside and top-stitching (page 30) close to the cut edge.

7 Hem the skirt bottom with a ½˝ single turned hem (page 51) or a ¼˝ double turned hem (page 51). Your choice of hem depends on how thick your fabric is and which method you're more comfortable with.

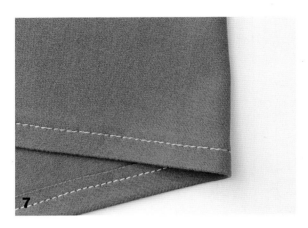

8 Switch the machine back to zigzag stitch. With the skirt inside out, place the bodice right side out inside the skirt so the right sides of the fabric are touching. Pin the waistline of the skirt to the waistline of the bodice, matching the side seams and raw edges. Sew a ½˝ seam in the round (page 50) around the circumference of the waistline.

9 Turn the dress right side out, press the waistline seam allowances open, and try on the finished dress!

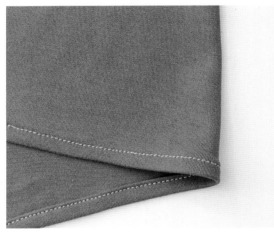

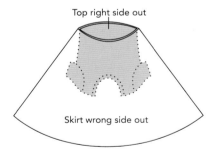

Top right side out

Skirt wrong side out

STYLE TIP

Since this style is pretty basic, you can always dress it up with some jewelry for something dressier. Try a statement necklace or gold hoops.

MAKE IT YOUR OWN

MAXI DRESS

Maxi dresses are fantastic pieces to have in your wardrobe during the spring or summer. They're easy to style and easy to wear. Paired with some wedges and sunglasses, you'll be good to go! In this variation, I modified the DIY Skater Dress (page 105) by cutting a rectangle of fabric the length I wanted my skirt to be + 1½˝ for the hem by the width of the fabric (instead of using the DIY Skater Skirt pattern). I then gathered it along the top edge, so it was the same measurement as the waist, and attached it to the waistline of the bodice. I also shortened the bodice so the waist would sit higher, shortened the sleeves into cap sleeves, and drew a higher neckline on the back piece.

DIY High-Rise Shorts

Now it's time to really challenge yourself with a pair of shorts. Not those basic PJ shorts they might have taught you to sew in school or at camp. These are actual shorts with a zipper instead of elastic! It's time to show off how much you've learned since the beginning. Make these in time for summer to show off your legs. Have fun!

FABRIC SUGGESTIONS

Choose a woven fabric with a little spandex—at least 2%. This will make the shorts a lot more comfortable to wear and move in. Medium- or heavyweight fabric with some stretch will work. The shorts need to have a little body, since they need to stand up to wear and tear (sitting and walking). I suggest denim, twill, wool, or even faux leather for some cool-girl shorts.

SUPPLIES

- Woven fabric with at least 2% spandex:

  45˝ wide, sizes XS–S: 1¼ yards   60˝ wide, sizes XS–S: ¾ yard

  45˝ wide, sizes M–L: 1½ yards   60˝ wide, sizes M–L: 1 yard

- 1 zipper:

  Sizes XS–S: 7˝ long   Sizes M–XL: 9˝ long

- A scrap of light- to medium-weight fusible interfacing at least as large as the waistband (page 19)

- Basic sewing supplies

- Thread to match your fabric

SKILLS CHECKLIST

The Basics (Chapter 1, page 9)

Patterns (Chapter 2, page 40)

Basic Techniques (Chapter 2):

- Pinning (page 47)

- Pressing Seams (page 49)

- Sewing in the Round (page 50)

- Hemming (page 51)

Seam Finishes (Chapter 3, page 64)

Advanced Techniques (Chapter 4):

- Darts (page 76)

- Inserting a Zipper (page 85)

Your creativity, style, and determination!

Shorts and pants are supposedly some of the hardest garments to fit because each body is different in terms of where the darts are placed and the exact curve of the butt (LOL). I encourage you to try on the shorts every step of the way, just to see if they're turning out the way you like.

CUTTING

Trace the DIY High-Rise Shorts Front and Back patterns (pattern pullout page P4). Cut them out to make your pattern pieces.

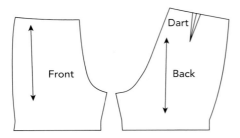

Prewash and iron your fabric. Cut out the pieces for your shorts using the cutting layout below. Remember to transfer the pattern markings!

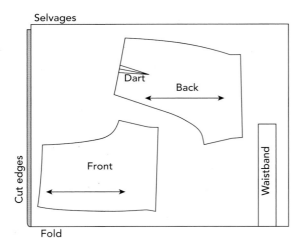

Cut 1 strip of fabric for the size you are making for the waistband:

  XS: 2˝ × 24˝

  S: 2˝ × 26˝

  M: 2˝ × 28˝

  L: 2˝ × 30˝

  XL: 2˝ × 32˝

Unfold the fabric layers and separate the pieces from each other. You should end up with 5 pieces total.

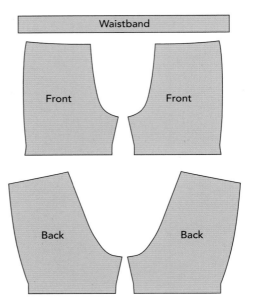

Cut 1 strip of fusible interfacing the same size as the waistband piece. Follow the interfacing manufacturer's instructions (usually on the packaging or on a strip of paper or plastic wrapped on the bolt) to fuse the glue side of the interfacing to the *wrong* side of the waistband piece.

Seam Finish

Zigzag over the raw edges of all the side seams of the front and back pieces before continuing. You don't need to finish the upper and lower edges of the front and back pieces or the waistband.

Sewing

Use a ½˝ seam allowance, unless otherwise noted.

1 Refer to Darts (page 76) to sew and press the darts on the 2 back pieces.

2 Place the back pieces right sides together along the center back/crotch seam. This seam is marked on the pattern. Pin and sew the seam.

3 Clip the seam allowances in the curved area. Press the seam open.

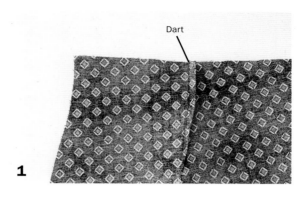

Dart

1

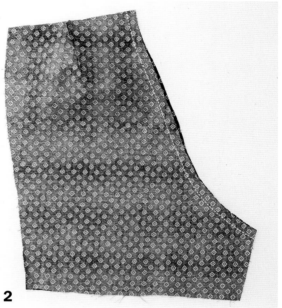

Clip.

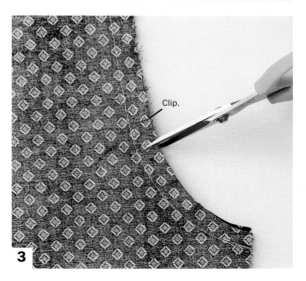

2

3

4 Place the front pieces right sides together and sew the center front/crotch seam. Clip the curved seam allowances. Press the seam open.

5 Pin the zipper to the center back seam, making sure to place the zipper pull ½˝ below the upper edge of the shorts to leave space for the waistband seam allowance.

If you haven't already, I highly, highly suggest you try on your shorts before continuing. Use safety pins to hold the unfinished seams in place. Be sure the waist is where you'd like it to be. If not, you may need to cut it shorter for a lower rise. Refer to Inserting a Zipper (page 85) to attach the zipper.

6 Put the back and front pieces right sides together, pin the side seams, and sew them together.

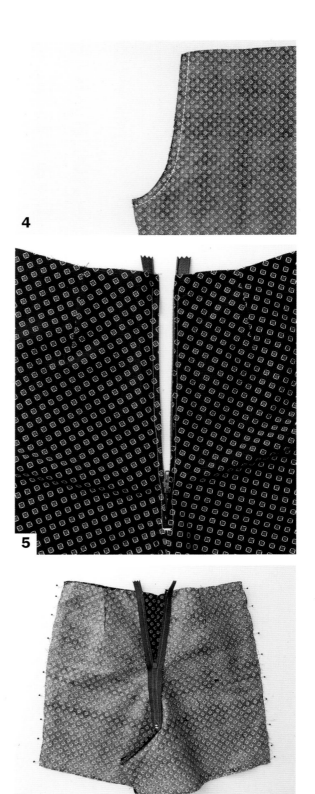

4

5

6

7 Sew the inseam (that's the short seam on the inside of each leg) of the shorts as a continuous seam. It will look like a U-shape, but pull it to make a straight line as you sew (page 49).

8 Hem (page 51) the shorts to the desired length or roll up the edge twice for a cuff like I did. You can machine stitch along the inner and outer side seams a bit to keep the cuff in place.

9 Fold and press both long edges of the waistband piece into the center, as if you were making bias tape (Step 6, page 84).

7

8

9

10

Starting from where the zipper opens, pin the waistband to the top edge of the shorts. Fold the short end of the waistband to line up with the zipper teeth. Sew, using a ½˝ seam allowance, all the way around. When you get near the opposite side of the zipper, fold the short end in again and cut off any excess fabric, leaving ½˝ folded over. Finish sewing the seam.

Shorts Front

Waistband

Fold

Shorts Back

10

11

Pull the waistband up away from the shorts. Press the seam, but don't press out the crease from Step 9.

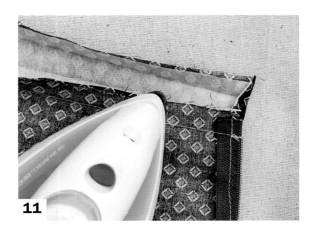

11

12 Fold the waistband down so the folded edge is just past the waistband seam. Pin in place from the right side of the shorts.

13 Working on the right side, topstitch (page 30) right along the seam to close up the waistband on the inside of the shorts.

14 Hand sew a set of hooks and eyes at the center back waistband where the top of the zipper ends. That's it!

12

13

MAKE IT YOUR OWN

HIGH-WAISTED SKINNIES

Skinny jeans/pants are all the rage and can look flattering on almost all body types. This pair, based on the DIY High-Rise Shorts (page 112), has a high waist and a wide waistband for a simple but classic look. Pants are the trickiest category of clothing to fit and make, so you have to be comfortable with advanced sewing techniques and pattern alteration.

To turn the DIY High-Rise Shorts into these pants, lengthen the side seams and inseams based on your measurements. As a special detail, I added decorative topstitching down the center of the legs by folding each front piece in half, wrong sides together, and sewing ⅛″ away from the fold. Try on your pants during each step so you can get an accurate fit and tweak the seaming if necessary. Transfer any alterations you make to your pattern pieces ("Take in sides 1″.", "Lower waist." etc.), so you can make many pairs in different fabrics and prints without worrying about the fit!

STYLE TIP
Zippers at the ankle of these skinnies would look darling and would help your feet get in and out of the tight pants much more easily. Follow the instructions in Inserting a Zipper (page 85), but line up the zippers with the ends of the outer side seams.

MAKE IT YOUR OWN

SWEATPANTS

Sweatpants are probably the most comfortable clothing to wear when lounging around the house, watching movies, or sleeping. You can style them many different ways.

I made these sweatpants in a soft and stable velour knit fabric by modifying the DIY High-Rise Shorts pattern (pattern pullout page P4) to lengthen the side seam and inseam lines, lower the waistline by 1½˝, add width/room to the legs by slashing and spreading (page 95), and sewing a contrasting-fabric ribbed waistband and cuffs.

STYLE TIP

Dress 'em up a bit with a leather jacket and bold lipstick!

WHAT'S NEXT?

What's next is to keep on sewing, of course! What you could make out of fabric and thread is endless, and now you know the techniques to do so! Experiment with different materials, switch up your style, and create different designs. Maybe there's a specific clothing item you like sewing the most and would like to learn more about it. Or maybe you're really looking forward to completing your dream wardrobe, which needs just a couple more pieces. In that case, you can buy different patterns at the fabric store and online. You have a variety of choices. There's a pattern for everything, from jeans to swimsuits to button-up shirts to skorts (skirt and shorts in one).

There are also many blogs dedicated to fashion sewing and style. Many of these are free-hand and "winging it," meaning sewing without a pattern, but that makes it so much more fun. You can learn to draw patterns by tracing existing clothing you own—or you can even draft your own from scratch. A couple of my favorite blogs are listed in Resources (page 126). Furthermore, you can find some of the most interesting and fun DIY clothing on Pinterest (pinterest.com).

I hoped you had fun during the course of this book. Remember to never stop DIY-ing! After all, a creative yet stylish hobby is a must. ;)

XX, ANGELA

GLOSSARY

Backstitching Sewing in reverse to secure the seam.

Basting Long, straight, temporary stitches; the longer stitches are easier to rip out than normal stitches are.

Bias The diagonal grain of fabric running 45° from the edges of the fabric; it has some stretch and "give."

Bias Tape Strips of fabric cut with the bias; used to cover raw edges or sewn on flat as decorative trim.

Bodice The part of the garment that covers the torso of the body, usually separated into "front bodice" and "back bodice."

Bolt (of fabric) The flat cardboard that fabric is wrapped around when displayed at the fabric store.

Center Front/Back An imaginary line running down the center of the front or back of a garment; often on a pattern piece it becomes one edge of the pattern.

Crosswise Grain The direction of the threads that are running parallel to the cut edge of fabric (perpendicular to the selvages).

Darts A triangle-shaped wedge pinched out of the fabric to create a three-dimensional shape that fits the curves of the human body.

Design Elements Choices made by the designer that create the look and shape of a garment and affect how it should be made.

Drape How fabric hangs.

Ease Extra room included in garments for comfort or style.

Fibers The materials fabric is made from.

Flare Fullness added to certain parts of a garment so it hangs away from the body.

French Seams A seam where the raw edges of an existing seam are concealed within the seam allowance by another seam.

Grainline An arrow on pattern pieces used to indicate in which direction the pattern pieces should be placed on the fabric; it usually runs perpendicular to the selvages unless a piece is to be cut on the bias.

Hem The lower edge of a garment where the fabric is folded to the wrong side to finish off the raw edge (on a sleeve, pant leg, bottom of a skirt, etc).

Inseam The seam on the inside of the leg.

Interfacing   A type of material used between the exterior and interior to stabilize or strengthen the fabric and add body.

Knits   Fabric constructed by interlocking loops of yarn or thread.

Lengthwise Grain   The direction of the threads that are running parallel to the selvages (perpendicular to the cut edge / crosswise grain).

Nap   Fibers on the surface of some fabrics that show a definite direction due to their length.

Notches   A small triangle or cut on the edge of a pattern piece or fabric to indicate where two pieces match.

Notions   Items used for sewing other than fabric, such as thread, pins, and buttons.

Pattern   A shape usually drawn or printed on paper used to cut out pieces of fabric to the same shape so a particular item can be sewn from the pattern pieces; there is also important information written on the pattern that is needed to sew it together correctly.

Raw Edge   The cut edge of fabric.

Seam Allowance   How far the seams should be sewn from the edge(s) of the fabric and how many inches should be added around the pattern pieces to compensate for the fabric lost when sewing a seam.

Seam Finish   Different methods used to prevent the raw edges of the seam allowance from fraying or raveling.

Selvages   The self-finished horizontal edges produced during manufacturing to prevent the fabric from fraying or raveling; often the fabric company, designer, and the individual color inks used will be printed on these edges.

Shoulder Seam   The seam that connects the front and back of a garment along the shoulder, running from the base of the neck to the end of your shoulder (where the arm starts).

Side Seam   The seam on the side of the clothing; on a top, it goes from the underarm to the bottom of the garment; on pants, the outer side seams are opposite the inseams; on skirts, the side seams are any seams on the left and right sides (like in the Skater Dress).

Tailor's Ham   A padded cloth-covered oval, shaped like a ham, used to press curved seams and darts to help shape them to the body.

Top Stitch/Top Stitching   Decorative stitching on the outside of the garment, often along the edge of a seam.

Wovens   Fabric constructed by yarns or threads run (woven) vertically and horizontally, alternating over and under each other.

RESOURCES

Fabrics and Notions
(IN ALPHABETICAL ORDER)

Eddie's Quilting Bee | **eddiesquiltingbee.com**
Though this is a quilting shop, they have an amazing selection of fabrics in their on-site store all suitable for making clothes—from luxurious silks to pretty voiles. I definitely recommend checking them out in person if you are in the San Francisco Bay Area.

Fabric.com
One of my favorite places for all kinds of fabrics and sewing supplies. The deals are great, and it's not hard at all to get free shipping, which is always, always a steal in my book. :) Many of the fabrics and notions used in this book were generously supplied by them.

Girl Charlee Fabrics | **girlcharlee.com**
This shop specializes in knit fabrics and has so many neat prints and designs. They're also starting to build their collection of woven fabrics.

Jo-Ann Fabric and Craft Stores | **joann.com**
My local fabric store and where I spend a ton of money (LOL). Visit their website to find a store near you and sign up for their newsletter to receive money-saving coupons.

Mood Designer Fabrics | **moodfabrics.com**
Where the designers of the show *Project Runway* shop. This store has the most gorgeous fabrics, and most of them are quite affordable, despite the amazing quality.

They also offer sewing classes at their Los Angeles and New York locations—some free!

Fashion/Sewing Related Blogs

LoveSpunk | **lovespunk.com**
This is my blog, where I write weekly and connect with my readers. I share style inspiration, beauty tips, lifestyle posts, and of course DIY fashion. I also have an entire Pinterest board dedicated to sewing your own clothes if you want more ideas and the best tutorials from around the web. Come on over and say hi!

Merrick's Art | **merricksart.com**
A fashion blog that also includes DIY clothing. I started reading Merrick's blog years ago and still love her sense of style. Her tutorials feature simple clothing that can be easily made, but with the outcome looking like they came from a boutique.

Cotton and Curls | **cottonandcurls.com**
For all those street-style and classy girls like me, this blog is for you. Liz has many tutorials on making your own clothes, especially dresses and tops. So it's the night before your big event and you still have nothing to wear? A simple but classy top or a 30-minute dress tutorial from her will do the trick.

Tilly and the Buttons | **tillyandthebuttons.com**
An incredibly helpful sewing blog with plenty of beginner to more advanced sewing tutorials. Tilly's step-by-step photos and instructions are great as a reference when you're stuck on a technique or just need a little more help.

Books to Check Out

Fairbanks-Critchfield, Caroline; Markos, Sarah. *Just For You—Selfish Sewing with Your Favorite* **SewCanShe** *Bloggers,* **Stash Books, an imprint of C&T Publishing, 2014**

Though not all about fashion sewing, there are a bunch of fun projects in here that are perfect for the beginner and intermediate sewist, including bags, dresses, skirts, and more.

Patch, Cal. *Design-It-Yourself Clothes,* **Potter Craft, 2009**

This a great book for those wanting to draft their own patterns from scratch or learn more about the pattern-making process. Cal explains how to draft everything from dresses to button-up shirts to pants. The book doesn't cover much on how to sew clothes from the patterns or garment construction, so a solid foundation in sewing will make grasping the concepts a lot easier.

Riegelman, Nancy. *Colors for Modern Fashion,* **Prentice Hall, 2006**

Everything you need to know about drawing, sketching, and color is packed into this book. It's quite hefty in price and weight, but I would recommend it to anyone serious about fashion design.

Smith, Nicole. *Skirt-a-Day Sewing,* **Storey Publishing, 2013**

An entire book on designing, drafting, and sewing skirts. Nicole teaches you how to create basic patterns (or "slopers," as professionals call them) and then transform those patterns into 28 different skirts. How cool is that?

For other great books and products, visit C&T Publishing at ctpub.com.

ABOUT THE AUTHOR

Angela Lan is a teen fashion designer and lifestyle blogger from Northern California. A self-taught sewist, she is an artsy girl who wants to pursue a career in design and start her own clothing brand. Angela writes weekly at lovespunk.com, sharing fashion and style inspiration, DIYs, and posts about the teen life, as well as a look into her personal life as a California girl. When not designing or blogging, she loves reading, traveling, shopping, taking pretty pictures, rocking out to music, and hanging out with her friends. She hopes to inspire you to live more fully, prettily, and happily.

"A beautiful image, a beautiful spirit, and a beautiful heart are all essential to be a beautiful girl."
—Holly Chen

INDEX